I Failed the UFE! Now What?
A survival guide

Kayla Switzer, MPAcc, CA

> "I know how it feels to fail, and I know what it takes to pass."
>
> - Kayla Switzer -
> Successful experienced UFE candidate

Dedicated to those who came before me, and to those who will follow, for failing the UFE and having the courage to try again.

"Failure is the condiment that gives
success its flavour."
- Truman Capote -
American writer

TABLE OF CONTENTS

Introduction — 9
Purposes — 11

Chapter One: December and January
I cannot believe I failed! Coming to terms with your results and determining the next step

Feeling emotional — 13
Understand you transcript — 15
Making sense of the results — 15
Analyzing your transcript — 18
Appealing and the PAR — 19
Signing up for Courses — 31
Getting support from successful experienced writers — 31
Going back to work — 32
Using your family for support — 33
What to do when people ask "did you pass?" — 34
Don't give up — 35
Traditional study schedule vs. non traditional — 36
Feeling Stupid — 36
Staying positive — 37
Identifying your weaknesses — 39
Chapter One quiz — 49

Chapter Two: February
Getting back on the horse

Plan of action for the year — 57
Studying details — 58
Traditional study plan — 59
Flexible Fridays — 59
Studying is different this year — 60
Pre study technical — 61
Pre study case writing — 62
Track your results — 64
Determination — 66
Interviewing successful experienced writers — 67
Courses and deadlines — 71
Statistics of experienced writers — 76
Study partners — 77
Studying alone — 81
Mentor — 82
Marker — 83
Firing your mentor or marker — 84
Markers: Big firm vs. small firm — 86

Chapter Two quiz	93

Chapter Three: March through July
And the studying begins!

Studying this year	101
Traditional study schedule	101
Study partner	102
Baby steps	102
Being an experienced writer	103
Psychologist	105
Stress	106
Anxiety	110
Keeping anxiety at a motivating level	111
Relaxation and vacation	113
Burnout	114
Sleep	115
Outlining	116
Debriefing	119
Module 6 and the Simulated UFE	123
Chapter Three quiz	129

Chapter Four: August
What to expect

Getting to Competent	137
Competency based marking	138
Have a routine	138
Stay on track	139
Lacking motivation	139
Don't study too much!	141
Being positive	141
Markers	142
Burnout and anxiety	144
Anxiety	145
Sports psychologist	146
Chapter Four quiz	151

Chapter Five: September
It's finally here!

Are you ready?	157
Last week of studying	157
Writing 2011 cases	159
One week to go	159
Weekend before the UFE	160
Monday before the UFE	161
Comprehensive exercise	162

Monday night before the UFE	163
Day One	164
Day Two	166
Day Three	167
Holiday!	169

Chapter Six: Results
Waiting (again) and the excitement of passing

Waiting	175
Making changes and staying positive	175
Getting a new job	176
You don't know whether you passed or failed	176
Results	178

Chapter Seven: The "supporters-of "
Make the people in your life read this!

Intro from a supporter	183
Giving support	185
The pressures of an experienced writer	185
No arguing	186
No evening or weekend study	187
What *not* to say	187
A schedule for you	190
Burnout	192
Day before the UFE	193
Day One, Day Two and Day Three	194
Holiday!	195
Waiting for results	195
Results	195

Chapter Eight: Experienced Writers
Real stories from real experienced writers

You are not alone	199
She did not give up	200
A male's point of view	202
She struggled to find a job	203
She had a reading disability	204
This Student Did Not Let Her Emotions Get in the Way	205
Successful third time writer	208
Contact	210

Conclusion	213
Notes	215
Acknowledgments	217
Appendix (Study Schedule)	219

"What lies behind us and what lies before us are tiny matters compared to what lies within us."
- Ralph Waldo Emerson -
American essayist, philosopher and poet

INTRODUCTION

Hello. My name is Kayla Switzer. On November 30, 2007 I woke up at 6:29 a.m. with anxiety and dread running rampant in my stomach. This was the day that I had been working towards for years, and all would be decided in thirty-one minutes. Had I passed? I grabbed my book from my bedside table and tried to read while my husband, Todd, sleepily patted my leg to reassure me that everything would be fine. He truly did believe that everything would be fine.

Todd didn't think there was any chance I had failed and leading up to the results he wasn't concerned. In fact, he was so sure that I had passed that when results came out he thought that there was a mistake on the website: that my candidate number had somehow gotten out of sequence, or that I was looking up the wrong number. As I lay in bed devastated that morning, he continued to get up and down to re-check the computer. I could see out of the corner of my eye that he was scrolling up and down, trying to determine if my number had somehow been put in the wrong order. He even phoned the institute to ask if there was a problem with the results. Todd believed so strongly that I had passed that he was the first to look again at 10 a.m. when the names were posted.

But there was no mistake. I had failed.

Leading up to the results I had been mildly confident that I had passed, but there was one nagging thought that was making me especially nervous. I felt like I had passed. Apparently, I had been told, that's not good. Working with my friend the week before he said; "I feel like I failed for sure, but I've been told that's a good thing. Everyone who thinks they passed ends up failing." Although I became mute from fear and didn't tell him the truth, the truth was frightening. I felt like I had passed.

Now, that's not to say that everyone who thinks they passed doesn't or vice versa. I worked with a woman who felt like she had passed and she was right. She got honour roll. I also worked with a woman who was positive she had failed, and she was right. She failed. But I was wrong. At 7 a.m. the marks were released and I had not passed. Competency Not Yet Achieved. I was devastated.

I know how it feels to fail, and I know what it takes to pass. I failed the UFE in 2007 and it felt awful. I thought I would never recover from the embarrassment and the disappointment of failing, but just one year later I passed the 2008 UFE and I felt accomplished, relieved, proud and inspired.

Everyone has the ability to pass the UFE, and I can help you discover how to recover from failing this year and pass next year.

You have this book as a resource. It will guide you through the process of being unsuccessful in December to success next December. And it's not just information on what to do; it's your personal resource guide for finding other resources as well. Use this book both when you need information and when you need to be reminded that you are not alone. You are not the only person to have failed the UFE! There have been many before you and many yet to come. In fact, 28.3% of writers across Canada (well over 1,000) failed the 2008 UFE. You are not alone! (The board has not provided pass/fail rates since 2008.)

This book is meant to provide you with all the information you need from start to finish after failing the UFE. I realized the need for this book within the first few weeks after getting my unsuccessful results, as the pain slowly began to subside. I had questions that nobody seemed able to answer, questions like: Can I appeal my results? Do I get to see my response? Do I have to do Module 6 again? (Applicable to CASB candidates only.) When do I start studying again? Should I start writing cases now? Should I have a study partner? Should I have a study partner who is also an experienced writer? When are the deadlines for signing up for everything?

My emails with questions were ignored, or I was told to hold-on and wait until the spring. My firm assumed that information provided to first-time writers was also relevant to my situation, but it wasn't. Many experienced writers need their questions answered much sooner in order to calm their nerves and prevent unproductive studying too early. Failing the UFE can create some pretty serious stress, so to move on without the right support and guidance on what to do next can be extremely difficult. In addition, as an experienced writer you have to consider which courses to take and you must sign up early, so without the right information you may not get into the courses you want to take. Planning the year will lessen the anxiety of the unknown, and this book will allow you to accomplish that.

During the spring and summer after failing the UFE I realized that the information that I was getting and the lessons that I was learning should not go to waste. Surely I was not the only person who found the lack of understanding of the needs of experienced writers atrocious. That is why I decided to document everything about my second UFE summer, my second attempt at the UFE, so that when I was successful I would be able to pass on all the information I had obtained.

Purpose

The purpose of this book is to provide you, as an experienced writer, guidance on how to approach writing the UFE again. I am passing on the information I received and the experiences that I had. Think of this as your survival guide.

"I Failed the UFE! Now What? An experienced writer's survival guide" is based on a month-to-month time line starting immediately after getting your unsuccessful UFE results in December and ending with passing the following year. Although nobody will have all of the answers to all of your questions (as each candidate has varied needs, experiences, and backgrounds) this book is a one-stop information source to get you started towards UFE success!

Believe in yourself. You can pass the UFE!

Helpful Hint: Read the entire book in December to get an overview of what to expect. Then re-read each chapter at the beginning of the time period that it relates to so that it is fresh in your mind. For example, Chapter Three relates to March through July, so I recommend reading the entire book now and re-reading Chapter Three at the beginning of March. At anytime you can easily refer back to any notes you have made. However, read and reread the chapters in whatever fashion works best for you because this is your UFE and only you know what you need.

"It's not that I'm so smart, it's just that I stay with problems longer."
- Albert Einstein -
Theoretical Physicist

CHAPTER ONE: DECEMBER AND JANUARY
I cannot believe I failed! Coming to terms with your results and determining the next step

Ugh...I Feel Emotional!

When I found out that I had failed the UFE I felt nauseous. All of the hard work that I had put into studying now seemed like a waste of time. I had worked diligently to be prepared and felt poised to pass, taking the game of the UFE very seriously. I honestly didn't know what I could do differently if I wrote it again.

The results day is a bit of a blur. I stayed in bed for what seemed like hours. I felt frozen. If I forgot for any length of time, when I remembered again a new wave of pain would flow through my body. I remember Todd phoning my family to say that I hadn't made it, and how crushed I felt to see the look on his face as he told them. I could easily imagine my dad's sombre expression and my mom's worried face. The phone rang all day, but I couldn't talk to anyone. I wanted to disappear under my covers and wake up in an alternate universe where I had passed the UFE and this was all a bad dream. Todd made me get up and get dressed and go for a bike ride. It was a cold, sunny day and we biked along the ocean and sat on the beach. I just stared at the water without really seeing it. I was silenced with fear. I didn't think I could write the UFE again, but I didn't want to quit either.

However, as the weekend progressed I began to feel more normal again. The thought of going back to work was becoming bearable, and I knew I would write the UFE again. I still felt miserable and dejected each time I remembered I had not passed, but I knew I could get on with my life.

Nobody close to me understood what I was going through and I felt very alone. After a few days Todd was unsympathetic because to him it was over and done and it was time to move on. I could write it next year after all! But for me it wasn't over and done, and I wasn't ready to move on. I was embarrassed. I was so embarrassed! And discouraged! Some days I felt like I would never be able to pass. I would wake up with a sinking feeling in my stomach. I felt discouraged and didn't want to see any of my friends with whom I had studied and written the UFE. In fact, it was months before I stopped avoiding them, and it wasn't until I passed the UFE a year later that I truly felt comfortable again.

Sometimes I felt like I was being too sensitive and that after a week I should have gotten over it; obviously worse things have happened to people. I felt like I was being very selfish to be spending so much time recovering from the embarrassment and discouragement of failing a test. "It's just a test" I would try to convince myself. But then I talked to other people who had been unsuccessful on the UFE and learned that it wasn't just me. It is true that some of the people that had failed didn't take it personally, and were confident that next year would be better, but they seemed the exception rather than the rule.

I didn't go to my firm's Christmas party that year. I had been to prior years' parties and I knew that the results would be publicly announced, and although my name would not be mentioned, the fact that it wasn't a 100% pass rate would fall heavy on my shoulders. Not to mention I would have to face all of "those people" who had passed. Although I am not proud to have felt this, I was jealous that it was them and not me.

I was severely affected by failing the UFE. Although it's not an advertised fact, most people are. Feeling this way is normal. It's important for you to know that the feeling of embarrassment, self doubt and discouragement is not an overreaction.

That being said, everybody is affected in their own way. There can be a whole range of emotions that unsuccessful UFE candidates go through starting with denial, then disbelief, then anger, and then you will accept it and move on. Everyone reacts differently, and the stages might happen at a different time for you than another candidate. Some people jump quickly to acceptance and start moving on almost immediately, so that might be you. Or maybe it will take you longer to get to acceptance than other people you know. It all depends on personality, and no one way is right or wrong. Personality wise we are all very different so how we react to failing will vary from candidate to candidate.

The key is that it is okay to feel bad and that someone who has not been through failing the UFE is never going to understand the depth of how you feel. The good news is that there are lots of people who have failed before! When your partners went through the UFE process the pass rate was probably about fifty percent! So you can always find support either within your firm, or by hiring someone to mentor you who has failed and passed successfully on a repeat attempt.

Results
Understand your transcript!

I explain the results below and what they mean. Understand your transcript, whatever it looks like, and know where you went wrong so you can improve next year. Doing this was key for me and helped ensure that I improved my weaknesses and passed in my second year. See Page 39 to learn about identifying and improving your weaknesses.

Making Sense of the Results

I was so confused by my UFE transcript. Because of the stress I felt from failing, it was hard to make sense of it. Clarity is always useful when you are in a stressful situation, and it's nice to have some help when you attempt to interpret the results, so I explain it all below. See my website for a sample transcript (www.KaylaSwitzer.com) and compare it to your own transcript so you can start to understand what your weaknesses are. Next year these weaknesses can become your strengths!

℞ *Remember: You can only improve on areas that you know are your weaknesses, so be brutally honest with yourself.*

Summary of Transcript
See my website for a sample (www.KaylaSwitzer.com)

The institute uses coloured boxes to reflect the overall result for each Level and sub-grouping of the level. Red for standard not met, yellow for standard marginally met, and green for standard clearly met. On the sample transcript on my website (www.KaylaSwitzer.com), the red box signifies that the candidate has not met the requirements of sufficiency (i.e. breadth across all of the indicators), the green boxes signify that the candidate has clearly met the requirements of Assurance, PM, GSRM, Finance and MDM, and the yellow box signifies that the candidate has marginally met the requirements of Tax, but nonetheless has passed Tax.

Helpful Hint: Note that the yellow box (Tax) is not what resulted in the candidate failing. It is the red box (Level One) that shows the result of a fail i.e. if the box for level one was yellow or green, the student would have passed the UFE.

Level I: Sufficiency

I failed at Level I. In fact, Level I is where most UFE candidates fail and where most experienced writers have to find their true weaknesses and correct them.

Essentially, sufficiency breaks down to the simple question of this: did you score enough marks overall. It does not matter where those marks came from in terms of competency area or Comprehensive versus Non-Comprehensive simulations. Level I sufficiency just records whether you scored enough marks to pass. A yellow or green box means that yes, you have scored enough marks overall, and a red box means that no, you have not.

If you did not score enough marks (you got a red box) you get a sufficiency rating. A sufficiency rating is a number representing approximately how many more times you needed to get Competent on a primary indicator, or increase your score from Reaching Competent to Competent on a primary indicator, in order to pass. Your sufficiency rating will be between 1 and 10, 1 meaning you were close to getting sufficiency and 10 meaning you were not close to getting sufficiency.

Scoring starts on primary indicators. For each Reaching Competent you get you are given approximately half the mark you would get on a Competent score. Candidates often fail at Level I as a result of not scoring consistently on primary indicators or not being able to write with adequate depth to score Competent ratings on a primary indicator. This can be a time management issue, because you might spend all of your time on the first two indicators of each case, and not enough time on the other indicators in the case, so even when you do really well on the first two indicators, you fail on level one because you are not hitting enough indicators.

Level II: Depth

Depending on the year, candidates have five to seven chances to score on Assurance or Performance Measurement and Reporting. All that matters here is how many times you get enough depth to score a Competent rating, i.e. a rating of Reaching Competence affects Level I Sufficiency but has no impact on Level II Depth; you can only pass Level II with Competent ratings. If you have a standard not met (red) in either of these areas then this is a weakness. You have a problem writing in sufficient depth to score a Competent rating on Performance Measurement and/or Assurance. It is also important to realize that there are two independent tests at play here: there is a test for Performance Measurement and also a test for Assurance. You have to get Competent enough times in both Performance Measurement and Assurance to pass at Level II.

It is never disclosed, and subject to change, but to pass Level II you probably need a minimum of two Competent ratings for each of Performance Measurement and Assurance. So think of it this way. A red rating is probably less than two Competent ratings, a yellow rating is probably two Competent ratings and a green rating is probably three or more Competent ratings.

Level III: Breadth

For the four competency areas covered by Level III Breadth, the issue is essentially this; did you score enough Reaching Competency ratings (or better) in each of the four areas? General rule of thumb is that you had to score 50% of the scoring chances you had. For example, if there were two primary indicators in GSRM then red means you scored zero times, yellow means you scored one time and green means you scored on both primary indicators. If there are three primary indicators then red probably means zero scoring, yellow would mean scoring once and green would mean scoring two or three times.

There have been occasions where it appears that a higher standard was applied and scoring two times was the minimum standard. In that scenario zero or one scoring attempt would result in a red rating, scoring twice would result in a yellow rating and scoring three times would result in a green rating. The same rules as this last example would likely apply in a situation where there are four primary indicator scoring opportunities.

Review of the Transcript
Analyzing the results

Level I Detail: Level I broken down

Sufficiency Grouping: This candidate is Sufficiency Grouping 1, so a small degree of improvement would pass them at Level I (i.e. scoring on approximately one more primary indicator.) However, if the sufficiency grouping was 6, the candidate would have been very far away from passing at Level I as there are normally only twenty eight to thirty two primary indicators to score on.

Decile Ranking on Comprehensive Simulation: This candidate is in the 7th decile, 70th percentile, or bottom three decile.

Decile Ranking on Non-Comprehensive Simulation: This candidate is in the 8th decile, 80th percentile, or bottom two decile.

The decile rankings explain where the student is in relation to all of the other UFE writers (successful and unsuccessful) that year. For example, the Gold Medalist would have been in the 1st decile, 10th percentile, or top decile with a decile ranking of one.

This candidate would have passed if Level I was yellow or green. The student has a weakness in sufficiency, and the consistent decile results indicate that there is an overall weakness, not just a Comprehensive approach problem or just a time management problem.

So, What's my weakness?
Understanding what your transcript actually means

In this example you would now start looking for what would explain not performing adequately on all three days. Maybe you were not comfortable with your approach strategy. Maybe you were not debriefing properly and never made the necessary performance jump. Maybe you did not wind down your study properly and burned out at the end. Maybe you have sleep issues. Maybe you did not manage your time properly (Level II and Level III results do not seem to support that in the example on my website, www.KaylaSwitzer.com).

If your transcript shows you passed at Level I but not at Level II and or III, then analyze based on that information. Use your results to start asking the right questions so that the real cause of failing can be identified.

When I failed I automatically jumped to the conclusion that I had to study longer and study more technical. But that is never the case. If you have a weakness in tax on your transcript it might simply be an issue of not attempting two tax indicators in a single simulation, or it may be a quantitative analysis problem, or it may be a specific tax technical study issue. You need to consider all of this, in addition to your writing style and study aspects, to find any weaknesses.

Appealing and the PAR

Below I discuss the appeal process and the Performance Analysis Report (PAR), which is an analysis of your UFE response. The cost of ordering either is quite high, so you need to weigh the pros and cons to determine if it will be beneficial for you.

D *Deadline: The deadline for appeals and ordering your PAR is typically the end of December so you have to make these decisions quickly. Appeal results are announced in early March. If you appeal your results and you are given a* *passing grade as a result of the appeal, the appeal and PAR costs are fully refundable, which is only fair!*

Moola
Show me the money!

The costs that you can expect are as follows (but subject to change):
- Appeal: $375;
- PAR: $500;
- If you order both: $775.

I Want a Recount!

I appealed my results when I failed the UFE. I didn't appeal because I thought that I deserved to pass. I appealed my results because there was a small, tiny, microscopic chance that there had been a mistake. I thought "What if it's a mistake that I failed, and I rewrite it all for nothing because I actually should have passed?" To feel peaceful studying all summer I needed to be fully confident that there was no chance of that. I had to be 100% sure. Only then would I be able to move forward.

I was fully aware that by appealing my results I was setting myself up for a repeat of the same feelings I had just gone through by failing, and that in the previous year the pass rate from appeals was less than 2%. I was also fully aware that the UFE responses are marked twice and if there are discrepancies between the marks they are graded again. But I needed to do it in order to move on, because the last thing I wanted during the summer was to be thinking, "Maybe if I had appealed my results I wouldn't be here at all." There was no way I would have been able to stay focused if I was pondering that. And so I sent in my appeal.

I found out that I hadn't passed on appeal by receiving an email at work one morning in late March. And so, one otherwise uneventful morning while sitting in a client's office, I opened up my email to discover that, once again, I had been denied a passing grade. Although I had tried to prepare myself, this second rejection was still difficult. I had made sure that I didn't get my hopes up over passing on appeal because the likelihood is so low. I assumed that I had failed and continued organizing my summer as if I hadn't appealed. However, there was always that small thought in the back of my head saying that maybe this is all for nothing. Maybe I won't have to write next year. And so, when I received the email, as prepared as I was for negative results, it was still hard. But it was now time to truly face my weaknesses and get into the mode of studying ferociously and passing the UFE once and for all. I have listed some of the pros and cons of appealing below.

Remember: In order to be able to decide whether or not you should send in an appeal, consider the pros and the cons. Make an informed decision. Talk to other successful experienced writers about what they did, but make sure you base your decision on what works for you.

Pros and Cons of Appealing

Pros:

1. You might actually pass!

2. It will put you at peace for studying.

Cons:

1. It's hard enough to be told you have failed once, and even more difficult to be told you have failed twice. After the pain of failing is finally wearing off, the appeal results arrive and you have to go through it again. This is difficult and emotionally exhausting. However, feeling like you failed again can be mitigated by preparing yourself and not relying on positive appeal results.

2. The chance of passing on appeal is very small, less than 2% usually, depending on the

year. If you have sufficiency grouping greater than 2 (see sample transcript on my website, www.KaylaSwitzer.com), the chance of passing on appeal decreases even more,
varying each year but often 0%.

3. It costs money to appeal, and the second UFE summer is extremely expensive, especially
if your firm is not picking up the tab again. I know mine didn't!

Who should Appeal?

Unfortunately, the chance of passing on appeal is very slight. In fact, almost nobody passes on appeal. The chance of passing decreases exponentially when your sufficiency at Level I increases, i.e. if you have Level I sufficiency of 10 vs. sufficiency of 1 your chance of passing is exponentially lower. So, unless you have a Level I sufficiency rating of 1 and no issues in Levels II and III, appealing *could* be considered a waste of money. There are probably better ways to spend your money, unless you need to appeal to be at peace. It's your decision of course, based on what you think will work best for you!

Remember: Read the material that comes with your unsuccessful UFE results. It has the information on appeal and PAR deadlines and processes.

Have your own ideas for pros and cons? Use the next page to write them down and make some notes to help make your decision easier!

Pros and Cons:

For more information on appeals, contact your local institute (see below for websites) or if you are in Western Canada email: appeals@casb.com

Canadian Institutes

Eastern Canada and Bermuda:
Bermuda: www.icab.bm www.icab.bm
New Brunswick: www.nbica.org www.nbica.org
Newfoundland: www.ican.nfld.net www.ican.nfld.net
Ontario: www.icao.on.ca www.icao.on.ca
Prince Edward Island: www.icapei.com www.icapei.com
Quebec: www.ocaq.qc.ca www.ocaq.qc.ca

Western Canada:
Alberta: www.icaa.ab.ca www.icaa.ab.ca
British Columbia and the Yukon: www.ica.bc.ca www.ica.bc.ca
Manitoba: www.icam.mb.ca www.icam.mb.ca
Northwest Territories and Nunavut: www.icanwt.nt.ca www.icanwt.nt.ca
Saskatchewan: www.icas.sk.ca www.icas.sk.ca

Should I Order My PAR?

I did not order my Performance Analysis Report (PAR). I was reprimanded by my firm for this, as it was their belief that I was not going to be able to improve if I didn't know what my previous mistakes had been. At first their reaction scared me. "Maybe I should have ordered it, maybe now I will fail," I thought. But then I reminded myself that nobody on the UFE Committee had written the UFE more than once and they didn't know my situation. After being very honest with myself and reflecting, I felt like I did know why I had failed and that I didn't need my previous UFE to teach me what not to do. I was nervous that instead of being motivated by seeing it, my PAR might do the opposite. I didn't want to take the chance of seeing my results and discovering that if I had done one thing differently I would have passed; this would have been demotivating and I didn't want to risk it. Because I was really honest with myself regarding my weaknesses, and because I was very close to passing the first time, I made the decision that the PAR was not right for me.

But that is not the case for everyone. Ordering the PAR is a personal choice that you should make based on your own personal style. Consider how you learn best, and decide whether to order yours based on how you learn, taking into account whether you think your mistakes will motivate you or discourage you, and whether you have someone who can help you review it (PARs are really confusing!)

Although I didn't order my PAR, I know a lot of people who did and found it useful to review their mistakes in order to learn from them, improve on them, and apply this to the next year. I know one man who failed on Level II because of Assurance. He ordered his PAR and discovered that if he had been clearer in his wording, he would have hit a particular Assurance indicator and ultimately would have passed the UFE. This motivated him to study his technical diligently all summer, focusing on the wording he was using while he wrote each case in order to hit these indicators. He received detailed feedback from ordering his PAR, allowing him to fully understand why he had failed at Level II (he had to improve his wording, not just technical knowledge), without which he may not have been as successful. He passed his second time. I also know several people who did not get value from their PAR, as it can be very confusing. However, students who have ordered their PAR generally tell me that they are glad that they did. If you are not sure whether it's right for you, ask some successful experienced writers what they did and ask them questions about how it helped, or why they wouldn't do it again.

There are many reasons why you should order your PAR, as discussed, and several reasons why it may not be useful for you. Only you know for sure. Nobody but you will know what's right for you, especially if they haven't had to repeat the UFE. Only you have the knowledge to make the decision. PAR's are very expensive and will not make any sense to you when you look at them yourself, so you will need to hire someone very familiar with that year's UFE to reorganize and interpret the results for you. A good PAR analysis requires a minimum of four hours analysis so it costs money, although some firms have someone in-house that can analyze it for you.

PARs are more useful the closer you are to passing at Level I. They are of limited benefit if you have a high sufficiency rating at Level I. They can also be very useful for identifying specific Level II problems. They are a very expensive way to figure out a Level III problem so if you failed at Level III you would be better served in that case to use the funds to hire a private tutor or marker.

Inside the PAR

To make your decision easier, I have summarized below what you can expect from ordering your PAR. This summary is to help you make an informed decision about whether it would be useful to you, and to summarize what to expect. The PAR consists of comments detailing what you need to work on based on simulations, competency areas, and professional skills, so although the price seems high at first, there is a lot of time put into it by the board to make it as useful as possible. That being said, it's not a necessary component of your study summer as an experienced writer.

The PAR is comprised of three sections:
Section A: This section is an indicator-by-indicator analysis of your performance by simulation;

Section B: This section is an indicator-by-indicator analysis of your performance by competency;

Section C: This section is a summary of general findings and analysis of your performance in several professional skill categories.

Section A: Analysis of performance by simulation

1. The reviewer lists the indicator and required;

2. Below the required an "X" denotes if the indicator was not addressed;

3. Below this, there is a list of what was not accomplished for the indicator. There is a paragraph to explain what would have benefited your discussion, and "X's" denote whether you demonstrated a flaw on certain items (e.g. Identification, Justification, Integration and/or Technical, depending on which items are relevant for the indicator);

4. At the end of this listing, there is a section for overall comments of the entire simulation. This explains whether there was a logical flow, you understood your role, the response was easy to read and understand, you prioritized primary indicators, and whether you had a balanced response with appropriate devotion to each indicator;

5. The reviewer may include additional comments that could be useful, e.g. "Your response could have been improved if you discussed the accounting treatment using fundamental accounting principles."

Section B: Analysis of performance by competency area

1. The reviewer lists the indicator and the colour achieved. Green for "Clearly Met", Yellow for "Marginally Met" and Red for "Not Met."

2. Comments from Section A are arranged by competency to summarize your competency strengths and weaknesses.

Section C: Summary of general findings

The general findings are listed by simulation and a brief note is made on each simulation for the "professional skills" (communication, prioritizing and ranking) listed below.

Communication:
- Was the response well organized with logical flow;
- Did you understand your role;
- Was the response easy to read and understand.

Prioritizing and Ranking:
- Was there appropriate focus on the primary vs. the secondary indicators;
- Was the response balanced.

The reviewer's comments are then organized by each "professional skills" category, as listed below:
- Identification of issue;
- Integration: Linking between response and case facts and/or within the response and/or between theory and case fact;
- Justification: providing adequate support for your position;
- Recommendation: providing advice to client when required;
- Technical sufficiency.

Have some ideas for why or why not to order your PAR? Use the following pages to write them down to help make your decision easier!

PAR:

PAR (Cont.):

Sign Up for Courses Now
The early bird gets the worm!

Due to the high demand of UFE courses I suggest signing up for an experienced writer's course as soon as you know that you are attempting the UFE again. Get on a waiting list if the course is already full. I recommend that you take the course at the beginning of your UFE summer (i.e. in July) to provide guidance at the beginning and get you back into the swing of studying. There is further discussion on courses in Chapter Two.

Getting Support
Ask successful experienced writers for help

The people you work with who are successful experienced writers themselves will be very understanding, especially in December when they know how fresh it is. However, sometimes even talking to experienced writers will be difficult. I was so stressed about my results that I couldn't talk about it without getting upset regardless of who I was talking to.

I had a manager who was a successful experienced writer. The week that I failed he told me that he understood and that he could help me if I needed anything, but I didn't want to talk about it yet. I also had phone messages and emails from several successful experienced writers, saying that they were available to chat when I wanted to. All of the outpouring of support was very much appreciated, even though I was not able to show my appreciation immediately.

Most firm UFE training programs are focused on the needs of first-time writers. The firm I worked for is one of the Big Four, so I thought that I would be provided with experienced-writer-specific support, but even with all the resources they have there was a deficiency for experienced writers. This means, unfortunately, that even if you get support from your firm you may still have to supplement it yourself. Seek out experienced writers who have been successful on the UFE and ask them for help and advice.

There are people in every firm that failed the UFE once, twice or three times, passed successfully on a subsequent attempt, and now it is behind them. These people are an extremely useful information source because not only do they understand what it's like to fail, they also have the knowledge of what you need to do to pass. Talk to as many of them as you can and most importantly talk to people who have failed and succeeded recently so that the knowledge and feelings are still fresh. Set up interview questions and invite them to coffee. Ask as many questions as you need to in order to get them talking and learn from them. They know what it takes to pass and you can learn from them. I explain this in more detail in Chapter Two on Page 67.

Showing Your Face at Work
Chin up!

Going back to work after I failed the UFE was horrible. The firm that I worked at didn't provide us with our own desks, which made it easy for me to hide from people I knew. Every morning I would search out a desk that was in an area of low foot traffic so that I didn't have to see people. In addition I didn't go to the Christmas Party, and I avoided talking about the UFE to anyone at work. It was mortifying knowing people knew and wondering what they thought about me.

Going back to work is difficult because you are surrounded by your peers. These people are either CAs, or even worse, have just passed the UFE that you failed. I was certain that everyone thought I was stupid. Although you may fear that people will think you are stupid, for the most part it isn't true. Several people reached out to me when I came back to work, and were nice about my situation. However, every office has a personality type that is unforgiving and who feels good knocking others down, so unfortunately you need to be prepared for someone who will take advantage of your situation, making you feel worse to make themselves feel better.

For me it was a manager who took every opportunity he could to reduce my confidence even further. He would try to be my friend in order to pretend that he cared about me, but then make rude comments with a smile on his face so that I wasn't sure what to think, or where I stood with him.

When I started working on being positive I realized that the way he was treating me was his way of building himself up. I was becoming confident enough through positivity to stop letting him put me down. Everyone comes across people in their lives who will try to knock them down, but only you can stop those people from affecting you by using your inner strength. You do not have to stand up to that person or become confrontational (although it may be helpful to confront someone if you think it will be effective.) Instead, focus on surrounding yourself with people who are concerned that you are okay and believe in you. Surround yourself with positive people and a positive attitude. See Page 38 for some of the exercises I did to regain my positivity after failing the UFE.

Thankfully, the negative type of person is less common than the people who want to see you succeed. The more common personality type in the office is one that you can reach out to, and those are the people you should search out. Tell them how you are feeling and get their input on how to succeed on this UFE attempt.

It is impossible to understand the pressure of having failed the UFE unless you yourself have failed it. Although there will be people you can reach out to, it is important to know that the pressure is often underestimated. Your firm and the people that you work with won't always realize that it may take weeks or months to recover from failing. Therefore, it is very important that you know what to expect and what not to expect. Discover who in your office is an experienced writer—you might be surprised! I guarantee that there are several seniors, managers and partners in every firm that had to write the UFE at least twice who will be more likely to understand your situation. Search them out so they can put you at ease.

Family Matters
So do friends…

Before I wrote the first time I had several people say to me "You've never failed a test before have you? Why are you concerned?" In all fairness, unless they are CAs themselves they cannot begin to understand. And even if they are a CA, it's probably been awhile since they wrote the UFE, so I'm sure by now they have tried their best to forget the work it took to pass the it.

If you are as lucky as me, you have a family that is sensitive enough to empathize.

Todd was amazing and I recommend being around someone like him when you fail; someone who thinks you should have passed but who loves you either way. For the first three days he was really supportive and understanding and okay with me being upset and feeling sorry for myself. By the fourth day when I arrived home from work disgruntled and upset, he was still relatively understanding, but was clearly near his end. And by the Wednesday after results day he had had enough. And so that Wednesday night he told me to "get over it", not six days after finding out my results. He couldn't understand, but I wasn't ready to "get over it." Luckily I have parents and sisters who agreed with me that I needed more time to "mourn" so they allowed me to talk to them, giving Todd a break from consoling me. Nobody has walked in your shoes and this makes it hard for them to empathize. But if you have enough support, there will always be someone there for you if you ask them to be. Be honest about how you feel with someone you feel safe with, whether it's family or friends, and who you know won't judge you. Only then can you get the support you need. You are not alone. Reach out and ask for help.

Of course, as I discussed earlier, everyone reacts to failing the UFE differently. The nature and degree of the reaction varies greatly from candidate to candidate, ranging from an intense reaction to the opposite end of the scale where the candidate is not strongly affected. If you have been extremely affected, it's okay, but try not to dwell for too long.

"Did You Pass?"
Please don't ask!

I had a lot of friends and acquaintances who didn't realize the significance of the UFE. They didn't know what a Chartered Accountant was let alone how hard I had worked to pass the exam. If someone says that they are writing The Bar Exam to become a lawyer, there is a certain awareness about how hard it is. It is more recognized and universally known as difficult compared to your average test. But the UFE is less recognizable, so fewer people understand its significance. If you are like me and have friends who simply don't understand, you are lucky if they just forget and don't even ask whether you have passed. However, most likely there will be a few people who ask you at some point during the year whether you have passed.

Now, the advice that I am about to give is nothing that you can't conclude on your own. But the whole purpose of this book is to help you understand that you are not alone, and that you are not overreacting, and that having the feelings that you are having is okay. When people ask, try having something clever or funny to say, and then change the subject. When people asked me if I passed I would try to make light of it and move on, usually after they had said something kind like, "don't even worry about it, you can pass next year." I always felt agony when this happened because I didn't want them to feel sorry for me, I didn't want to talk about it, and the only thing people could really say wasn't comforting. Unfortunately that is part of the process of failing the UFE.

Don't Give Up!

It's easy to feel like you should just give up, or wonder if you have made a mistake by deciding to do your CA. But don't give up now. You have come this far and one more summer of studying, although it seems like a monstrosity right now, is only a drop of time in relation to the rest of your life. Enjoy the idea of spending another summer on your own schedule with no boss but yourself. Take advantage of the summer, and make it your best yet!

For example, you can study in the morning and have afternoons to enjoy the summer sunshine. I studied from 8 a.m. to 3 p.m. in my second UFE summer, so every day when I had finished studying I went to the pool or the beach to lie in the sun. This made me feel like I had every afternoon off and made studying less of a chore. I actually enjoyed my second UFE summer more than my first, because I was more in control and confident. I knew what my weaknesses were, I knew I was working really hard, and I knew I was focusing on dealing with stress. I was also much more positive. I wasn't just *trying* to be positive (which is what I did the first year) I really was positive.

R *Remember: Don't give up yet. When results first come out and you are feeling low it's easy to get down on yourself. But think of the positive side—you don't have to go to the office this summer!*

Clarification in the Confusion
The traditional study schedule vs. what's right for you

After reading this section, several students have come to me confused. When are you supposed to follow the traditional approach, and when do you not? I studied from 8 a.m. to 3 p.m. Is this right for everyone?

In general, candidates are told to follow the traditional study plan which starts at 9 a.m. and will wrap up around 4 p.m. (Most experienced writers never make it to 5 p.m. and do not need to.) The actual UFE starts at 9 a.m. so starting your studying all summer at 9 a.m. is strongly encouraged because you are training yourself to "win the game"! Starting your studying at the same time as the UFE starts will train your brain to be ready to write at the same time every day.

I totally and completely support this traditional study plan, even though I myself started at 8 a.m. For most people, starting at 9 a.m. is the best choice. Some candidates, including myself, can modify the basic study plan and still succeed. However, you tend to decrease your chance of passing the more you deviate from the traditional plan. So don't modify the plan without a lot of thought and research. If you think the traditional study plan isn't right for you, don't make that decision on a whim. Think about it! Discuss it with other writers who have been successful in the past, and make sure that any changes you make are based on what's best for you. For me, it was more important to start early and enjoy my summer. I adapted the study schedule accordingly, and it worked really well for me. But I didn't decide on a whim. I talked to a lot of people and did a lot of thinking before I set my study schedule, and that's what worked for me. That's what was right for me and worth the risk of modifying the traditional study approach. But it's not right for everyone, so do not modify it without some serious thought about the risks and rewards. If you aren't sure, then go with the traditional study plan starting at 9 a.m.

Am I Stupid?

No! After failing you may question yourself about whether you are stupid and whether passing the UFE is even possible. Whether you failed at Level I, II, or III, or all of the above, you are not stupid. We all have good days and bad days or nerves that we can't shake, but this doesn't change the fact that you can pass the UFE, and you will. This is your year!

It is not unreasonable to get down on yourself and feel frustrated, but by January it is time to start thinking positively. By thinking negatively, you will only set yourself up for failure because nobody can pass the UFE if they think they are stupid. It is impossible to pass thinking this way. The UFE is more a test about your ability to handle stress, anxiety and the psychology of a big exam than about the content itself. Yes, of course you need to know your technical, have a good writing style and know how to identify issues and triggers, but if you got this far you are capable of passing the UFE. The big issue is thinking positively.

Bring back your positive spirit. You were smart enough to get this far, so you are certainly smart enough to pass the UFE.

I Think I Can, I Think I Can, I Think I Can…
I know I can! Stay Positive.

I went between feeling excited and very apprehensive about studying again. I was excited to get started with studying and just get on with it, but at the same time I was scared. I had this nagging feeling: what if I can't do this?

When I started feeling that way I had an exercise that I would go through. As soon as I started doubting whether I could pass, I would go through a list of reasons that reminded me that I could. Depending on where I was at the time I would either run through them in my head, re-read my list that was stuck on my fridge, or write them down again to reinforce them. I suggest that you make a similar list of things that you can repeat to yourself when you start feeling apprehensive about your ability. You can pass the UFE! Don't let your mind get the better of you because if you think positively you have won half the battle.

Here is the list that I used to remind myself to stay positive.
1. I know what my weaknesses are and I know how to make them my strengths;
2. I have made it this far, I can pass the UFE.
3. I can do this, I just have to put my mind to it. I have the power to pass the UFE!
4. Lots of people pass the UFE every year. If they can do it, I can do it!

Use the remainder of this page to write down a few of your own positive reminders, and remember to refer back to them if you start feeling negative.

_____
_____
_____
_____
_____
_____
_____
_____
_____
_____
_____
_____
_____

Identifying Weaknesses
Why did I fail for f*#k sake?

When I failed the UFE I didn't feel like I could have done anything differently. I truly believed that I had done everything that I had been told would lead to my success. How was I going to pass with my second attempt? It felt impossible.

I had been told that I should write down my weaknesses and what I needed to do to improve my UFE results. At first I wanted to scream! I mean, how should I know? If I knew, wouldn't I have done it last year? But then I just started writing down anything that came to mind. I came up with a list containing several things that might have led to me failing the UFE, and although some of them seemed somewhat minor (Weakness: I was dehydrated. Action: Drink more water) they were all issues that I could improve upon to lead to my success. By digging deep and being totally honest with myself, I realized that there were several key things I could improve on.

Listing Your Weaknesses

There is nothing more frightening than having to acknowledge your weaknesses. I tend to believe this is especially hard for accountants who are typically very hard on themselves and don't want to fail at anything. To admit that they have done something wrong is admitting that (gasp) they're not perfect! Now, that's not to say that accountants won't admit that they have faults out loud. I've heard many accountants admit their faults out loud. However, of those same accountants I have on several occasions realized, after digging deeper, that the fault they have just divulged is actually a strength! This certainly does not count as truly acknowledging your weaknesses.

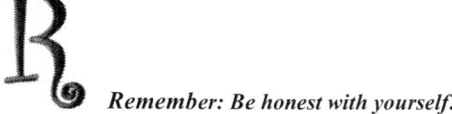
Remember: Be honest with yourself!

You are not the only one who finds admitting your weaknesses to be a difficult task. Admitting your faults is an art that we don't all excel in. However, it is absolutely mandatory for succeeding in passing the UFE because you must understand your weaknesses that led to failing in order to improve on them and successfully write the UFE next year. So, yes it will be hard, but it simply must be done. And be specific. If you're too general you won't be able to improve on it. Here is an example:

Too Broad
My Weakness: I didn't debrief enough.
ACTION: Do a better debrief.

Clearly it would be difficult to improve on this because there is no "what?" and no "how?" What was weak about your debrief? How should you improve your debrief?

More Specific
My Weaknesses: My debriefing was weak.
- I always focused on what I was doing well on and spent too little time on what I was doing wrong.
- I didn't track my results in enough detail.

ACTION: Have a strong debrief and track in detail.
- When debriefing, focus on indicators that I get Not Addressed and Nominally Competent
- Have a clear understanding of why I didn't get to Competent.
- Document it in my notes so I can understand my weakness and improve on it the next time the issue comes up. If I do not improve the next time, consider why. Did I forget? Do I not understand? Put a post-it at my desk/on my computer, so that I can be reminded of my weakness and reach Competent next time.
- Consider a rewrite of that indicator if I continue to forget.
- For indicators I get Reaching Competent on, review to see what I needed to get to Competent and make notes I can look back on. Do the same thing for Nominally Competent and Not Addressed (i.e. know where I went wrong and take notes so I can improve.)
- For indicators I get Competent on, review them to ensure I know what I did well on so that I continue to do well!
- Track by indicators and sub-indicators so that I have enough detail to know

what I am improving on and what still needs work. For example, I will document what I get on a tax indicator under Personal, Corporate, Section 86, etc. instead of just "Tax". By keeping this detailed tracking, I will be able to see what I need to improve on within a particular indicator, instead of too generally (i.e. "I keep getting Not Addressed in finance" is too general. Be specific. What kind of finance issue? Cash flow, covenants etc.) (See the discussion on tracking on page 64.)

For every major weakness you identify, list the weakness in detail and make an action for it, using the example above for guidance. Find a format that works for you. If you are a visual person, then make it visual. Read over it every day for the first couple of weeks of studying in August to make sure you remember to do what you have promised yourself. Keep it on-hand throughout the summer so that you can refer to it even in September to make sure you feel confident that your weaknesses have been addressed and are becoming your strengths.

What are your Weaknesses? How will you address them? Use the following few pages to list them and determine an action plan so you can refer back to them often.

Weaknesses and action points:

Weaknesses and action points (Cont.):

Weaknesses and action points (Cont.):

CHAPTER ONE SUMMARY

Failing is devastating. You feel alone. There are decisions to be made in December and January (Should I appeal? Should I order my PAR? What courses should I sign up for?) and it's hard to stay organized. But not anymore! Follow along with Chapter One and you'll be right on track.

Failing sucks, but by the time January comes around it's time to move on. Use this chapter as your action plan. Below I have included a checklist so that you can be sure you haven't missed anything.

December and January Checklist:

1. Read the entire book "I Failed the UFE! Now What? A survival guide."
2. Review your results and have a clear understanding of what level you failed on last year. If you don't understand your transcript in great detail, ask someone for help! (You can email me through my website at www.KaylaSwitzer.com if you have questions!)
3. Sign up for a course in July to start your UFE summer off strong.
4. Appeal your results. (Not mandatory. Deadline is specified in your results letter, but likely is at the end of December.)
5. Order your PAR. (Not mandatory. Deadline is specified in your results letter, but likely is at the end of December.)
6. Create a "positive" list to run through when you start feeling like passing next year is impossible. See Page 37.
7. List your weaknesses. Make an action plan to help define how you will study this summer. Be specific and honest! See Page 39.
8. Accept that you have failed, and then move on. This is your year to pass the UFE!

Have other action items for December and January? Use this page to write them down:

December and January action items (Cont.):

December and January action items (Cont.):

CHAPTER ONE QUIZ: WHERE ARE YOU EMOTIONALLY?

Read the following questions and answer as honestly as possible on a scale of 1 to 5. (1 = Never 5 = Always)

1. Do you find it difficult to say out loud "I failed the UFE"?
       1   2   3   4   5

2. Do you wake up and dread going to work?
       1   2   3   4   5

3. Do you feel like giving up?
       1   2   3   4   5

4. Do you break down in private and/or at work?
       1   2   3   4   5

5. Do you feel like everyone thinks you're stupid?
       1   2   3   4   5

6. Are you skipping firm functions because you are too embarrassed to see people?
       1   2   3   4   5

7. Do you find it more difficult to fall asleep and/or sleep through the night than before UFE results?
       1   2   3   4   5

8. Do you find yourself unable to list your weaknesses and feel like there is absolutely nothing you can do differently next year?
       1   2   3   4   5

9. Do you find it difficult to discuss the UFE with colleagues and/or your family?

                                1   2   3   4   5

10. Do you find it difficult to think positively about being able to pass the UFE next year?

                                  1   2   3   4   5

RESULTS: NOW ADD UP YOUR POINTS AND SEE WHERE YOU FIT IN BELOW.

If your score is between 10 and 24 points: *You have accepted that you failed the UFE and you are ready to move on—or are you indifferent to failing?*

Accepting you have failed and having confidence in yourself to move forward is absolutely necessary to be able to approach the UFE again and succeed. If you have approached failing the UFE with the realistic view that although it sucks, you are not going to let it get you down and you are ready to study "smarter" and pass next year, then good for you! But is that true, or are you simply indifferent to having failed and are just going through the motions of writing the UFE again?

Your Exercise: Answer the questions below. Be honest with yourself. Ensure that you are in the right space emotionally to pass the UFE.

1. **I know I failed and that sucks. I was upset at first, but onward and upward!** If this is how you feel, then great. You are going to have the confidence you need to pass the UFE!

2. **It simply doesn't bother me that I failed. I'll try again next year; it's not the end of the world. I never felt that upset about it.** If this is how you feel, then proceed with caution! Indifference is not going to be enough to get you through the UFE. Don't misunderstand. I'm not saying you have to be an emotional wreck in order to be able to pass the UFE. However, indifference often means that you aren't facing your real feelings. Dig deep. How do you really feel? Is it really that it doesn't bother you? Or is it something, like fear for example, that you just don't want to deal with? You want to be able to have confidence so that you have the ability and mind-set to be a successful UFE candidate next year, but you need to make sure that it isn't fake confidence. If you are indifferent or faking confidence, you are not going to have enough drive to make it through the UFE.

1. If you have concluded that you really aren't upset, that this is great news! Let's move on!

2. If you have concluded that you aren't facing your feelings:

Your next exercise: Find a quiet space either in your house, in a park, or alone in your car, and think. Start by asking yourself the following questions, and see how it makes you feel. Come to a conclusion and take action to build true confidence.
- Why don't I care?
- Am I truly unafraid of the consequences of having failed?
- How has failing affected me?
- Am I ready to move on or do I just not want to accept that I failed?

If your score is between 25 and 39 points: *You are starting to accept that you failed and with a little more work you're going to have the confidence you need to pass the UFE and get on with it! Good for you! Although you are still feeling upset about failing sometimes, you are working hard to be more accepting of your situation and know that you will get through this.*

Your exercise: Don't give up. Keep working on staying strong and accepting your situation. Having confidence and staying strong emotionally is more than half of the battle! See Page 38 for an exercise on staying positive.

If your score is between 40 and 50 points: *You are struggling emotionally. You are still struggling to accept the results and are having difficulties moving forward. You are not sure what went wrong or where to go from here.*

Don't worry if you are still feeling this way. It's still early in the year, so you still have time to start thinking positively and to train yourself to accept the results and move forward. You need to dig deep and understand why you are feeling so distraught, and then pull from your inner strength to become strong and secure. Work on this for the next few months and by the time you start studying again in the summer you will be able to say out loud "I failed the UFE."

Your exercise: Find a quiet space either in your house, in a park, or alone in your car and think. Start by asking yourself the following questions and see how it makes you feel. Try to come to a conclusion about why you are feeling how you are feeling and how you can draw confidence from within.

- Do I feel overwhelmed? If so, maybe you need to start organizing your summer and take action, so you can feel more in control. (Read Chapter Two and Three for guidance.)
- Am I afraid to accept that I failed and move on, because I think that means I'm not taking failing seriously? If so, you need to take control of your anxiety and accept that getting over your fear and gaining confidence doesn't mean that you're not taking it seriously. (See Chapter Three regarding your anxiety.)
- Do I feel like there is nothing I can do this year that I didn't do last year? If so, you need to make a list of everything, as little or big as they seem, that could have been a weakness last year and dissect it. This will help you to understand your weaknesses and make them your strengths! (See your list in Chapter One on page 43.)

Have your own ideas about how you are feeling? Use the following pages to write them down, along with what you can do to take action!

December and January - ideas, feelings, action:

December and January - ideas, feelings, action (Cont.):

"I've missed over 9,000 shots in my career. I've lost almost 300 games. Twenty-six times I've been trusted to take the game-winning shot...and missed. I've failed over and over and over again in my life. And that is why I succeed."

- Michael Jordan -
American professional basketball player

CHAPTER TWO: FEBRUARY
Getting back on the horse

Plan of Action
Get organized, but don't start studying yet!

By February it is time to get started with planning. In fact, some experienced writers will want to start planning before this point, which is fine. Keep in mind: being organized is important but don't stress yourself out unnecessarily, especially this early. Planning is appropriate, but actually starting to study this early is not.

Don't start studying now! That will just set yourself up for failure!

R *Remember: This chapter will guide you towards organization, but actually studying doesn't start yet! Don't study more this year, study smarter.*

When I wrote the second time I wanted to start writing cases in January but I was told by a couple of people that this was not a good idea, that it would lead to burnout and I would be sure to fail again. I certainly didn't want to fail again, although not studying immediately did take some personal will power!

It is important to keep everything in perspective because it's easy to feel like you need to start studying as soon as possible. Repress that urge! Studying too soon can lead to burnout, fatigue, and ultimately to another failed attempt. In my second summer I wanted to start studying right away, so I understand if you do too. But I also know that this is a stressful time. You have just failed the UFE and busy season at work is in full swing. It may feel like it's time to get started again…but slow down.

I have included a sample study plan in the Appendix on Page 219. On the following pages I discuss studying in more detail, and what it's going to be like this year.

Studying
The details

Everyone has different lifestyles, different ways of studying and different ways of de-stressing. While the study plan in the Appendix (on Page 219) is the traditional study plan, the recommended study plan, and the perfect plan for most, make sure you adjust it so that it works for you if necessary. Talk to other experienced writers and ask them what they did, how long they studied for, and gauge their learning styles compared to yours. This will help you to tailor the plan so that it's perfect for you, if need be, because although this traditional study schedule works for most people, there are some people that it's not right for. For example, I met an experienced writer who had followed the guidelines of studying morning to evening the first summer and failed, and so the second summer he set up his schedule so that he studied later on in the day, which was how he had studied in university with great success, and he passed the second time. Studying every day consistently is very important, regardless of your schedule. But if you think the traditional study plan isn't for you, consider what might be better to meet your lifestyle and your learning style.

Remember: The actual UFE is written in the morning at nine, so it's a good idea to be on a schedule similar to this if possible, as this will help you to be productive for the actual exam.

Your study schedule should incorporate writing one UFE worth of cases on your own before July (spread between March and June), a course in July and personal studying of four weeks in August and September. The number of weeks you study should represent your learning style. For example, I need time to take things in and learn, and I need to be able to have the time to rework things over and over again for the concepts to stick, so I studied for six weeks plus a one week course. However, for most people six weeks of studying is way too long. Especially if you are an individual who learns quickly and picks up concepts without having to do a lot of reworking, then less studying will be more reflective of your study requirements.

The Traditional Study Plan
Don't deviate from this without serious consideration!

Most successful experienced writers take a ten day to two week UFE preparation course in July and have four weeks of independent concentrated UFE study in August through September. Research has shown that the optimal study period is four weeks of independent study. Candidates performance when they study for four weeks versus five weeks consistently have better results. The chances of passing decrease dramatically once you study more than five weeks. In the UFE process, more study doesn't mean better results. Study smarter, not more! Although it worked for me, I was the exception. So this is what I mean when I say you have to do what works best for you.

The basic study plan that works for thousands of writers each year is 9 a.m. to 1 p.m., break for lunch, and then study again from 2 p.m. to 5 p.m. Actually, most experienced writers study to 4 p.m. and never make it to 5 p.m.

Helpful Hint: You don't need more than one course in the summer. One course in July plus your independent study is all you need, and anything more than that will contribute to burnout, which decreases your chances of passing.

Flexible Fridays

In the study schedule I have provided in the Appendix on Page 219, I have incorporated "flex days". Friday flex days are comprised of one simulation in the morning with the afternoon open to study whatever you want to work on.

Some candidates do not write any simulations on flex Friday and focus just on technical review or other aspects, and some candidates choose to write and debrief two simulations, maybe rewriting one or two that they didn't do well on during the week. Most candidates, however, balance that day with one simulation and some technical study. The key aspect about flex days is that it gives you the ability to work on weaknesses that come up during the week and address them, keeping your stress level low by addressing any issues, and leaving the weekend without anything left on your "to do" list.

R *Remember: Flex Friday doesn't mean take the afternoon off to go to the beach (unless you're burned out, in which case taking an afternoon off is never a bad idea). Flex Friday means that you have a few hours before the weekend to deal with any struggles you had during the week, so that you go into the weekend feeling strong! Don't leave Friday afternoon without dealing with your weaknesses.*

H *Helpful Hint: It's important to have lots of fun non-UFE events in your schedule. Plan camping trips, dinners, tennis matches, board game nights—whatever it takes to make it a fun summer! Write these events into your study schedule so that you can see them on paper and have something to look forward to!*

My Study Schedule Looks Different This Year…
It is!

This schedule is probably different from your schedule last year. I know it's different than my first year and that's because this year is different. You are an experienced writer now so you don't have to cram in as much information because you know it already. It might not feel like that at first, but soon you'll notice that a lot of it is just review.

Also, in my first year I wrote the Comprehensives on Tuesday morning because that is the day of the week for the Comprehensive on the UFE. But in my second year I wrote them on Mondays, because although the day of the week is not the same as the UFE it is still the first case of the week, which more accurately simulates the feeling of the first day. Also, in my first year I debriefed the Comprehensive the same day I wrote it, but a Comprehensive takes five hours to write, so it is not reasonable to debrief it in the same day and learn from it. You are too tired for that. Instead, mark it on Monday afternoon so you know how you did, and debrief on Tuesday morning. The traditional study plan is to write the Comprehensive on Tuesdays, so you decide what works best for you.

Pre-Study Technical

The study plan in the Appendix (on Page 219) includes technical study in the months approaching your study summer. This is not an opportunity to study rigorously and memorize all of your technical, it is simply a light review. It has been a long time since you studied full-time for the UFE, so a lot of the technical will need to be refreshed. If you start writing questions with no review it will be difficult to identify issues, which will be frustrating. The purpose of this light review it to help you identify issues when you start writing cases again, allowing you to feel more in control. You should not expect to know all of the technical after the review. The detail will come from writing cases and doing detailed debriefs when you start to write.

I have put the technical study on weekends; however it is not necessary that you do the work on a Saturday or Sunday. I found that I preferred to do it during the week after dinner, allowing me to have my weekend to myself.

Remember: You are coming off of busy season at work. If fitting in technical review is too stressful, then don't do it. It is not mandatory. If it stresses you out, then it is working against the plan of trying to prepare you for the UFE. If you don't get to study your technical in the spring, you will be able to learn it in the summer while you are studying.

The basic experienced writer study plan has three components and does not start until March. You are a year more experienced and on larger jobs at work, so you have to survive busy season. It is not realistic to think you will do effective study in those peak work times (January and February) so do not create unneeded stress by scheduling it in when you won't be able to do it.

Technical study is normally done in the period between March and June. Realistically you are going to have four to six study hours per week at the most, which is not enough to do all of the studying you want to do so you need to prioritize. Your technical study should focus on the technical issues that you know always come up on the UFE for all six competency areas, so that when you arrive at your UFE preparation course in July you have a good base of technical knowledge.

To help you prioritize you can use the knowledge lists at the back of the competency sections in the competency map or you can use Kathy Wolfe's UFE Competency Map Notes, which is also a good study source. Last year you wrote four years worth of UFE's when you studied (plus you wrote the UFE!) so you should have an idea of the technical that is almost always tested. If you're not sure, start looking through the competency map and you might surprise yourself at how many topics you recognize as being regularly tested. Use this knowledge to sort topic areas into "Must know", "Nice to know" and "Don't need to know" categories. Then study by priority and across all competency areas. By the time you get to your UFE preparation course you will not know everything, but you will know the high priority topics. By having this technical knowledge you can focus on other important skills at the course, instead of worrying about technical.

Pre-study case writing

I have also added to the study schedule in the Appendix (on Page 219) six Non-Comp simulations and one Comprehensive to be completed before your course in July so that you have been able to complete one full UFE before getting into full-time study mode. These have also been scheduled to be done on weekends, but doing them during the week allows you to have the weekends off, and depending on your personality, may be less stressful. Please modify the schedule in whatever way is necessary to ensure that you are meeting your needs and learning in your most efficient and effective manner.

I suggest writing a simulation every two weeks between March and April. Write a simulation one week and get it marked, then debrief it the next week. This will keep the hour requirements realistic for any given week. Since you will be writing three non-comprehensive simulations over an eight week period it also reflects the reality that there are likely going to be a couple of weeks when work commitments will preclude any UFE study.

In mid to late May you should write, get marked and debrief a Comprehensive case. Get it done early enough before your July course so that you can get feedback and learn from it. In mid to late June you should write a four hour three simulation Non-Comprehensive examination under exam conditions.

Some firms require you to write simulations during the spring that are then marked for you before studying begins. If this is the case, include these as part of the pre-study "UFE." For example, when I was in my second summer of studying I only had to do two cases on my own, as I was required to do several for the course put on by my firm. It is easy to integrate firm requirements into your overall study plan and an effective way to include non-UFE cases. The simulations that you do between March and July should not include any of the cases you will be writing in August and September. In August and September you will be writing all of 2008, 2009, 2010 and 2011 so these simulations should not be written before August. You don't want to use up valuable UFE material now, as you should be using it to study later.

Remember: Between March and your UFE course in July, you will write a full UFE; a total of one Comprehensive and six Non-Comprehensives. Writing a full UFE over several months before you start studying will remind you how to write UFE cases, get your stamina back for sitting for long exams, and refresh you on how to debrief.

Helpful Hint: Debriefing properly is the key! See Page 119 in Chapter Three for details on how to properly debrief so you can get comfortable with it in the spring. I cannot emphasize enough the importance of a strong debrief. There is no point in writing cases if you are not debriefing and learning from your mistakes.

Tracker
Stay on top of your results!

You need to track your results from the very beginning. Each time you write a case, starting from the very first one you write in the spring, track what type of indicator it was and how you did. And be specific. Don't just say that it was a Tax Indicator for example. What type of tax?

Here's how to set it up. Use an Excel spreadsheet and along the top label each column. Have seven sections for each competency area. Within the seven sections, have a separate column for different *types* within the competency area. So for example, Tax might have Section 86, Estate, Personal, Corporate and any others you find relevant. For Pervasive you might have Fraud, Unethical, Bias, Independence, Overall Conclusion etc. Do this for each of the seven sections, with each sub section in it's own column.

The two columns on the far left should have the headings "Date" and "Case". Every time you write a case you input the date you wrote it, what case it was, and then input what you scored under the appropriate column. For example if it was a question with Performance Measurement, Assurance and GSRM and you got Reaching Competent, Reaching Competent and Competent you would put those three results in the sub section column that most accurately represented each.

The final step is to calculate the mark. You can expect that Competent garners approximately twice the marks that Reaching Competent does. So in the example above with two Reaching Competents and one Competent you would get a mark of four (one mark for each Reaching Competent and two marks for the Competent) so you would have scored 67%, because the total possible mark is six.

Reviewing Your Tracker
Make good use of it!

Calculating the percentage is a helpful way to see your improvement from week-to-week. At the end of each week, calculate the average results you got that week to make sure you are improving. Sometimes you won't show improvement, which is fine as long as you go back and see where you struggled and what to work on next week.

I always summarized and calculated my weekly weakness by calculating my percent that was less than Reaching Competent, i.e. all of my Nominally Competent and Not Addressed. So for each of the seven competency areas I would summarize my marks showing the total number of Competent, Reaching Competent, Nominally Competent and Not Addressed I got. Then I would calculate my percentage for each competency area that was less than Reaching Competent. For example, after a couple of weeks, in Finance I had one Not Addressed, three Nominally Competent, two Reaching Competent, and one Competent. So out of a total of seven Finance indicators I had four that were less than Reaching Competent, or 57%. So clearly, this is something I had to work on. But I didn't stop there.

Knowing I had to work on Finance I went back to my tracker and looked in more detail. What type of Finance indicator was I weak on? What specifically was my weakness? Notice that it wouldn't have been much help if I had just said, "I'm weak in Finance. I have to work on that next week." That is not specific enough, because where on earth would I start?!? Instead I went back and saw that within Finance, the two sub sections I was weak on were Bank Covenants and Financing, that those were the two areas I was having trouble hitting. So I knew very specifically what I needed to work on.

Determination

You failed the UFE. So did I. So did a lot of people. And you know what…nobody cares. When you have "CA" behind your name nobody is going to ask you how many UFE attempts it took. In the scheme of everything it just doesn't matter. So there is no point in hurting your chances by hanging your head in embarrassment. This will hinder your chances of passing by lowering your confidence. Hold your head up high. Remind yourself of the prize at the end of it (you will never have to write the UFE again and you will be a CA!) and move on!

It was hard for me to move on. I just didn't know how I would ever get over the embarrassment and get the determination I needed to be a successful UFE writer. I was not only embarrassed, I was unsure of whether it was even possible for me to pass! Looking back, I realize that this was my "undetermined self" talking. In hindsight, of course I could pass, and so can you. If you feel like it's impossible, then consider everything you have done for school and work to get this far. It is absolutely impossible to get this far in your career and not have the ability to pass the UFE. And the flow-through rate of almost 100% is a testament of this. But it took more than seeing the flow-through rate to get me determined. It took a real hunger to pass the UFE.

That real hunger was pointed out to me by a manager at work. He was a successful experienced writer and suggested that I should have someone in mind, someone to motivate me, i.e. someone I wanted to prove something to. He suggested maybe I wanted to prove that I could pass either to someone who had never believed in me or someone I looked up to. The idea was that I had only so much motivation within myself, and maybe I needed a final boost of determination.

I didn't get along well with this particular manager. I decided right then and there that he would be my motivation. I wasn't going to let him put me down again like he had the first time I failed. This year I was going to pass and really surprise him. I would prove to him that I could pass the UFE.

Although this may seem like it's a negative way to get through, I actually found it quite positive. It allowed me to remind myself that he was wrong and that I was good enough to pass the UFE and smart enough to become a CA. It reminded me that only I could decide where I ended up in my life, and for me that was passing the UFE and getting my CA. Essentially, I took a person who was negative about my ability to pass the UFE and turned him into an empowering way to obtain confidence and accomplish my goal. And so I was determined.

After a few weeks, I didn't even think about this manager again or my goal to prove him wrong. The determination I felt morphed into feeling determined; he had just given me the extra boost I needed. And there were other things that motivated me of course, not the least of which was that I had worked hard to come this far, and I wasn't going to quit without my CA!

To pass the UFE you need to believe that you can. You need to be determined. You need to have your game face on and make it the most important summer of your life. Do whatever it takes to have the determination you need to pass. By the end of the spring and the approach of study season, it will be time to get over the embarrassment of failing and become determined.

You can pass the UFE!

Interviewing Successful Experienced Writers

There are four main reasons that I passed the UFE: I had a very supportive family who believed in me and helped me believe in myself, I went to a sports psychologist who helped me deal with anxiety over the UFE (I had a lot of anxiety!), I had a fabulous mentor, and I interviewed as many successful experienced writers as I could. Interviewing experienced writers was one of the keys to my success because hearing about other peoples' experiences helped me to prepare myself for what to expect.

I cannot stress how important it is to interview experienced writers. Why recreate a plan when you can get first-hand experience from someone who has gone before you? Mostly you won't have to beg because experienced writers tend to have a soft spot for other experienced writers, but if you have to beg, do! Do whatever it takes to take as many experienced writers as possible out for coffee (at individual times) and pick their brains. Have questions ready ahead of time and get them talking freely if you can, because that's when you will get the most information. Interview anyone who has written the UFE more than once and been successful. Make sure that some of the people you interview have passed within the last one to three years so that they are as close to the process as possible. It's important that they still have a good understanding of the UFE, as it does change from year to year.

I had a list of questions that would differ slightly for each person I interviewed based on what I knew about them. I would start by asking a few questions and that was usually enough to get them talking openly. All of my questions were usually answered without me having to ask them all, as the open dialogue covered everything I had thought of and usually a lot more. I would also ask them for suggestions of other people to interview, which was a great way to be introduced to people I didn't know and increase by "database" of experienced writers.

Examples of Questions I Asked

This list is not comprehensive, it is simply meant to get you thinking about what questions to ask. Remember to ask several different people all these questions, and then meld their answers together to determine what is right for you.

1. Did you take a course in July? Which one? Do you recommend it? What have you heard about other courses?
2. What is the best time to take a course?
3. Did you have a study partner? If yes, was it an experienced writer? If no, how was that? Which do you recommend?
4. Where did you study? Was it a good location?
5. Did you have a marker?
6. Was your mentor an experienced writer?
7. How many weeks did you study?
8. What do you think is the one major reason you passed?

Use the following pages to write down the questions you want to ask!

Questions for successful experienced writers:

Questions for successful experienced writers (Cont.):

Courses and Deadlines

For both Eastern and Western Canada there are several courses that you can take that help with the process of getting back into the game. I won't discuss them here, mostly because I do not have enough background to discuss the pros and cons of each. However, suffice to say that if you search Google for UFE related material, there are several options. I will mention this: I did have the privilege of working with Bruce Densmore, and I can honestly say that sitting with him for just one hour in May before I wrote my second time, helped me pass the UFE. Bruce knows the UFE and understands the process so well, and he is genuinely passionate about writers being successful—and he has a particular interest in helping those of us who have to write it more than once. I was not able to attend his Experienced Writers Course, however I have heard from everyone who did that it greatly increased their confidence, which is the key to passing the UFE.

I did however take the course that my firm provided in July, which was the perfect way to get me back into the UFE mindset and start my study summer off strong. If you are in a Big Four firm they will likely hold a training course for UFE writers. Depending on the firm they vary in length and detail, and are typically mandatory for first-time and experienced writers. Even if it is not mandatory as an experienced writer, I suggest taking the course. I found my course much more useful as an experienced writer. I was already familiar with the material so it was a good review (because I understood it more deeply) whereas the first summer I felt like it was too much to absorb.

You can take a course that is aimed specifically at experienced writers (Densmore Consulting Services Inc. has a course aimed at experienced writers, and there are others as well) or you can go to a course that is general UFE prep that is attended primarily by first-time writers.

I encourage you to consider the benefits of taking a course that is held specifically for experienced writers. The advantage of being in a room that is full of people just like you who have failed the UFE and are back this time to do it again is invaluable. You will have more support in this environment. I have spoken to several people who feel that the reason they passed on a repeat attempt was the confidence they got from going to a course for experienced writers.

Time, money and logistics do come into this decision. Currently, experienced writer's courses are typically held in Toronto so if you do not live in Toronto, flying to Toronto and getting a hotel for a week and a half is required over and above the cost of the course. Obviously monetary considerations weigh heavily on many UFE decisions for experienced writers. Ultimately though, it's passing that matters. Attending a course that will help you obtain the skills and confidence to pass should not be a decision of whether there is enough money in the bank. It is a decision of whether you require that resource.

Deadline: Deadlines for these courses are typically later on in the spring, but don't be fooled by dates. They all fill up very quickly due to the high demand, so get your name in there at the beginning of December. There are other deadlines that you need to consider as well, all of which depend on where you are in Canada. I have broken it down into Eastern and Western deadlines below, so read the section relevant to you and make your decision.

Eastern Canada and Bermuda

Deadline: <u>Experienced writers course:</u> There is no mandatory course for you to take. ASCA candidates have to take a finalist course on their last attempt, but not necessarily the ASCA Finalist Preparation Program. Attending a course in July is highly recommended. You are not required to redo SOA or CKE (that's a relief right!) However, there is no sense trying to do this alone. Passing the UFE is a hurdle that is not accomplished on one's own. The guidance and support of those who have come before you is the key to your success. There are several courses available to experienced writers and these should be taken advantage of, so search them out now, know the deadlines, and sign up.

Deadline: <u>UFE sign up:</u> The deadline to sign up for the UFE is typically in late July or early August. The exact date varies, so for the application form and deadline go to your provincial institutes' site.

Western Canada

Deadline: <u>The Complete Module 6:</u> The deadline to sign up for Module 6 is typically in March. They are very strict about the deadline, so make sure that you decide whether you want to take it, or not, early on. If you do, make sure you know the deadline. The deadline and application form can be found at www.casb.com. If you do not sign up on time your application will be subject to late fees and you will only be able to participate if there is room available at your location; you may be put on a waitlist. It is not required that you redo Module 6. CASB offers Module 6 section-by-section to experienced writers, so you can choose the elements that you need.

In my second UFE summer I didn't take the complete Module 6, and most candidates don't. I knew that I could learn more by studying on my own because that is my learning style. I know of several experienced writers who have taken Module 6 on a repeat attempt, although in every instance I know of, it was not with success. Module 6 is focused on learning how to write UFE questions, something that you have already learned in your first UFE summer. There is little focus on confidence and weaknesses, which is typically what you will need to focus on as an experienced writer. It would be more effective to take a course that is geared to experienced writers.

Deadline: <u>The Simulated UFE:</u> The deadline for signing up for the Simulated UFE is usually in March. Similar to Module 6 you will be charged late fees if you apply late and will be put on a waitlist if there is not room for you. So know the deadlines and sign up on time. Information can be found at www.casb.com.

I knew that I would benefit from being in another exam situation before writing the UFE again, so I signed up to write the Simulated UFE. This also meant that I wrote simulations on the two Fridays that the Complete Module 6 was held and had my cases marked. You will be familiar with this as it is the same structure that you would have gone through the year before, when Module 6 was mandatory. Doing the practice exams and the Simulated UFE was beneficial for me, and helped me to feel confident in the UFE exam situation. I felt prepared when I wrote the actual UFE because I had sat through the Simulated UFE already, so the nerves of writing were less of an issue.

Although I wrote the simulated UFE, I don't recommend it for most people. The cases written by CASB are not representative of the UFE, so it is only in rare instances that the simulated UFE is worth writing as an experienced writer. I only recommend taking the Simulated UFE if you feel anxiety when writing tests, and especially when writing the UFE, and only if you are aware that the cases do not represent the UFE. You are purely writing the cases for the exam experience.

Helpful Hint: Although the Simulated UFE is a great way to recreate the environment and make it feel like a familiar situation when you are writing the actual UFE, the cases are not representative of the UFE. The requirement to obtain Competent on the Simulated UFE is not reflective of what is required to obtain Competent on the UFE. Therefore, if you do write the simulated UFE do not spend much time debriefing it. The cases are written and marked in the UFE style so it is easy to confuse them with UFE cases, but they are more technical and less Big Picture.

Therefore, although you should take the notes provided by the markers seriously and review them briefly, I do not recommend putting a substantial amount of time into debriefing.

The Simulated UFE
In summary

The downside risks of burnout and inappropriate feedback on the simulated UFE outweigh any benefit of simulating the three days of the UFE. If you are going to write a simulated UFE as an experienced writer, have a very clear vision of what you expect the benefit to be and what the risks are. If I were to write the UFE again, I don't think I would do the Simulated UFE again.

Deadline: <u>On-line portion of Module 6:</u> This is available only to experienced writers, and is only for those experienced writers who have not signed up for Module 6 as it is included in the Complete Module 6 package. Having access to the on-line portion provides you with all the UFE reports, technical study, and other exercises provided on the website similar to what you had access to in the first year. The deadline for signing up for this is in August, so you have time to consider whether there are other resources for you to acquire all of the old UFE Reports and whether you want to have access to the website for the extra resources. Information can be found at www.casb.com.

The on-line portion is helpful in two cases: you don't have any of the UFE Reports, or you used the technical study notes the year before and found them useful. I had enough study material including my collection of notes from my previous summer, the Densmore Consulting Competency Map Study Notes, and the Handbook, so I didn't need the additional CASB notes from the website. I hadn't looked at any of the study material on the website in my first year, so I didn't think I'd have time my second year either.

That being said, there are some study packages on the CASB website that you might find useful, and they do update them every year. I personally feel that there is not enough time in your study schedule to take advantage of these packages, and that if you do it is likely to lead to burnout. But if you feel like you benefited from those resources the first year, or if you feel like that would be a valuable addition this year, then you should sign up.

Deadline:<u>UFE sign up:</u> CASB typically requires that you are signed up by the beginning of June. Late submissions are not accepted so make sure your application gets in on time! The date changes each year so check www.casb.com www.casb.com and look for application forms and deadlines. Additionally, check out your provincial institute websites for the applicable deadlines.

Statistics of Experienced Writers
You will pass!

The statistics say that you will pass. Flow-through rates are as high as 98% after three attempts so the statistics speak for themselves. If you are wondering whether you have what it takes to pass the UFE, think about that 98% flow-through rate because statistics don't lie; you can pass the UFE. There is no reason to believe that because you failed the first time, or the second time, or the third time, that you won't be able to pass this time, because that is absolutely not the case. You have done all of this before. You know what to expect! Use this experience to your advantage and boost your confidence. Remind yourself that you have already studied all the technical, so a lot of it will be review this summer. You have also felt the jitters of writing the UFE already, so this time the feeling will be familiar and therefore less scary.

Remember: As an experienced writer you have more experience

than the first-time writers because you have already gone through everything that they are about to go through. You have a head start. And you are a resource for them. Just because you failed the first time won't deter them from asking you for advice. Be open to this; it will increase your confidence by reminding yourself how much you know.

Everyone can pass the UFE. If you have made it this far, all it takes is a belief in yourself. Don't allow yourself to talk negatively about the UFE. When someone talks about the UFE to you, don't use language like "if I pass" or "I could easily fail again." Being positive starts from saying it out loud and eventually you will believe it yourself, because it's true. You can pass the UFE. You will pass the UFE.

How to Study and the Study Partner Conundrum
Do what works for you!

When I failed the UFE I felt very alone. All my friends had passed and here I was right back at the beginning signing up for the UFE, studying my technical, and taking another summer off unpaid.

I didn't know who I should study with. I didn't want to study with someone I didn't know, but I had been told I shouldn't study alone. I did know some people who had failed, but I didn't want to study with them, and I didn't know if it was okay to study with a first-time writer.

Of the few experienced writers I knew within my firm, I didn't really want to talk to them about studying, and I could tell they felt the same way. We danced around the subject of failing for several months and rarely discussed our study plan or how we felt. We were embarrassed about not passing and didn't especially want to talk about it. Each one of us had a different plan for the summer, and we mostly kept it to ourselves. There was one woman rewriting that worked at my firm who I considered studying with, but we decided that it wouldn't work. Our study locations of choice didn't agree (one of us would have had a long commute) and we both had a different study schedule. She planned to start studying quite heavily at the beginning of June and I didn't want to get burnt out. She was certain her study style required that she break from UFE tradition and study for three-and-a-half months. Unfortunately she was unsuccessful.

And then there were first-time writers. I didn't think that a first-time writer would want to study with me! I mean, I had failed and who would want to study with someone who had failed? After talking to several successful experienced writers during the interview process, I learned that it's quite common for experienced writers to study with first-time writers.

There are some drawbacks to studying with a first-time writer; primarily that at the beginning of the summer they will be behind where you are, which may lead you to spend more time helping them and less time on your own weaknesses. This will put you behind where you might otherwise be because you will likely be spending valuable time teaching them. Another disadvantage is that it might be discouraging if you are studying with a first-time writer who is very strong, because if you feel like they are doing better than you at the beginning of the summer this could discourage and demotivate you, which is dangerous. Additionally, a first-time writer won't understand what it's like for you on a repeat attempt and depending on their personality, might be less supportive than an experienced writer.

That being said, studying with a first-time writer can be a positive experience as well. You are experienced in technical and debriefing, however it has been a long time since you did it so it will take some time to get into it again. If your study partner is a first-time writer, you can re-learn by explaining to them. For example, explaining your debriefing style will refresh it in your mind and make it more clear for you and your study partner. First-time writers also tend to have higher confidence about passing, and will keep your spirits high.

In the end I chose to break with the traditional study recommendation and I studied alone. This is against all the "UFE Rules", and I was initially very nervous about it. I would not have decided on my own to study solo for my second UFE summer, because I wanted to follow the rules and I was scared about the consequences of not following them. But the more experienced writers I spoke to, the more I understood that I needed to study the way it worked for me. I believe that you need to follow the "UFE Rules" but it's also important to do what feels right for you, and sometimes that means you have to break the rules.

I spoke to several experienced writers who had studied on their own successfully and who stressed to me that it works for some people but not for everyone. One successful experienced writer suggested I have a study partner that I could study with on occasion in the case that I got bored studying alone or if I started to have motivation issues.

And so, for my second UFE summer that is what I did. My friend and I made a plan that I would study with her and her study partner once or twice a week. However, as it turned out I studied on my own all summer. I got into a nice rhythm and I enjoyed studying on my own. I had always studied alone at University because I learn better that way, so although I had planned to meet up with my friend I never did. However, I am glad that I made those plans because it was always in the back of my mind that I could go and meet her if I wanted to.

In addition, in the first year I found it very inefficient to mark my study partner's responses, and did not get any substantial benefit from it. My opinion is that marking your own responses is much more efficient, leaving more time to study technical at the end of the day. Improvements in writing technique should be made based on notes from your markers.

I do realize that telling you that I studied alone all summer and that I passed the UFE is vastly removed from all the advice you have ever received. And I don't want to confuse you. Please understand that I do not disagree that having a study partner is a good idea, and I cannot stress enough that it is especially important for anyone who lacks motivation or has a hard time getting out of bed and to the library in the morning. Be honest with yourself and if you need someone to be waiting at the library to make sure you get out of bed, then you should by no means be studying alone. If there is a chance that you will blow off studying because you don't have someone waiting for you, then you need a study partner. Although I myself found marking my study partners papers inefficient, I had a marker who marked several of my papers. So another reason to have a study partner is if you don't have a marker so that you can trade papers with your study partner on occasion.

I spoke to numerous experienced writers who had been forced into having study partners in the first year but because they didn't thrive in that environment decided on no study partner in the second year, which led to their UFE success. I spoke to one man who was a successful second-time writer. He had been an honours student in Math and Science in University but failed the UFE the first time. For him he was certain it was because of the studying. His personality didn't allow for him to be studying for seven hours straight with a study partner because he started to get fidgety and was unable to register what he was learning. In the first year he said that he would sit in the library with his study partner for the allotted time, but was unable to concentrate or retain the information. The second year he studied for the UFE the way he had always studied in University, which included long breaks between writing cases. This was significantly different from what his UFE mentors suggested to him, and he was given strict orders by his firm to follow a more consistent study plan, but he didn't agree with them, and noticed a vast improvement in his cases and continued to study in his own way. He was successful on his second attempt and went on to become very involved in UFE mentorship and marking. His story is vastly different from every suggestion that is made to UFE writers about studying. Studying in the recommended UFE format and with a study partner is still suggested; what I have told you above doesn't change that. I too recommend that you have a study partner and that you study consistently and as though it is your job from 9 a.m. to 5 p.m. I certainly do not recommend that you write a question and then take a couple hours off before debriefing it; under most circumstances this is not the most productive study manner for the UFE and it would make me nervous to do that. However, I also do not recommend studying in the UFE recommended format if you cannot learn from that type of studying.

My point is this: although following the "UFE Rules" leads to success for almost everyone, there are a few people for whom all the rules do not work. There are some people who work better studying alone than with a partner, and some people who work better studying with a partner than alone. There are some people who can sit for seven hours straight and learn well and some people who simply cannot sit for that long. You need to determine what works for you and study in such a way that allows you to pass the UFE.

R *Remember: Only you can decide what is best for you. Be honest with yourself and don't make the decision lightly. Talk to successful experienced writers and ask them what they did, and get an understanding of what worked for them and whether it will work for you. But regardless of what you choose, make sure you have a marker, whether you hire someone or you switch with your study partner on occasion.*

I studied on my own and I was successful. I may have also been successful if I had studied with a study partner, but I'll never know. What's important is that I weighed all of my options, discussed it with successful experienced writers, and made the decision based on a lot of information. You need to think about how you have always studied in the past, whether it has been successful, and use this information to determine how you should study for the UFE. And always have a marker! You need to know that you are marking yourself accurately. You need to have someone else reviewing your papers so that you can compare their marks to yours, and if you're not marking yourself correctly, find out why. If you're marking yourself too easy then you risk not debriefing in enough detail, and if you are marking yourself too hard you might lose confidence because you will feel like you're never getting to Competent.

Studying Alone
Clarification in the confusion

I always have students ask me about this, because everyone in the past has always told them they cannot, under any circumstances, study alone. What I say above is important to consider because there are candidates who break the "UFE Rules" and succeed, like myself. Studying alone is what worked for me. Unfortunately, breaking the rules and studying alone often leads to failing. Most candidates, especially experienced writers, have confidence issues. If you are studying by yourself then you are comparing your responses to the evaluation guide, which is not possible to reproduce. Most candidates studying by themselves start to have confidence issues after two to two and a half weeks and start second guessing themselves because their responses are not the same as the evaluation guide. The UFE requires confidence and determination and once a candidate loses sight of what is realistic, their responses stop improving. Unless you are extremely confident in your own abilities it is hard to rebound from that.

Having a study partner or a study group is not only about getting you to the library. A big benefit of a study group is to get the occasional independent marking, as I discuss above, and to be able to discuss questions about the guide. Candidates tend to be too easy or too hard on themselves when they mark their own responses, so it is helpful to have someone mark your responses sometimes to ensure you're on the right track with your marking. You can also use the group to see how others do things better than you so that you can incorporate that aspect and improve your own performance. Study groups provide a knowledge base, so you can ask each other questions about technical or skills issues. A good study group will challenge all members and raise their overall performance.

Studying in a group didn't work for me, but on average deviating from studying with one or two people is not in your best interest, so sticking with the traditional plan is recommended unless you are extremely confident that you will do better studying on your own.

UFE Mentor
Find an experienced writer to mentor you

I had an amazing mentor who was so dedicated to me. Having just passed the UFE on a second attempt herself she was very understanding and helpful. I definitely owe a lot of my UFE success to her. I didn't know her well before I asked her to be my mentor; she just fell into my life and I am grateful for that.

I wasn't sure who to choose as a UFE mentor. In my first year my mentor rarely returned my phone calls, not because she's not a nice person (she's a very nice person) but because she's so busy. She's the person at the firm who people look up to because she works really hard and she's great at what she does, but that doesn't necessarily translate to a good mentor. In my first year I chose her because she had been on the UFE honour roll and she had a lot of experience marking, so I thought that having her as a mentor would be a great chance for me to get some good advice, but it wasn't. When I was struggling with Performance Measurement at the end of my first summer I asked her for help and all she had to say was that I would be fine, and that I was going to do really well. That was great to hear, but in hindsight it wasn't that helpful. I needed someone to walk through the approach for Performance Measurement to make sure I was addressing it correctly. So, in the second summer I chose an experienced writer who understood my situation and she was amazing. When I didn't feel confident about my progress, she had me send over some examples and she provided me with detailed feedback on how to improve.

You are responsible for finding an effective mentor. If you are not getting what you need from your mentor they need to know, and if it doesn't improve then find another one. It was not my mentor's fault in the first summer that I didn't get enough from her, it was mine. I wasn't clear about my needs. However, I did learn from my mistake and in the second year I was very particular about what I needed. I needed someone who learned in a similar way to me and who had passed the UFE recently on a repeat attempt.

Over that summer my mentor was so dedicated to me. She would spend full weekends pouring over my cases and marking them, providing me with suggestions of how to improve my writing style and giving me examples of Assurance procedures. One afternoon in August I remember doing terribly on a case and I felt broken, which started a negative spiral. How was I going to pass the UFE if I hadn't the first time? Why was I bombing cases? I phoned my mentor, and although she was in the middle of work she talked me through it. She didn't want me to get negative, she said, because there was no way I could stay focused if I did. She reminded me that it's not realistic to think I would do well this early in the summer. I can't remember everything she said, but it made me feel better. And what is important is that she understood how I felt. Just one year before she had been in my shoes and knew how unnerving it could feel. The ups and downs that I was feeling she had also felt.

Having a mentor who understands is so important. Therefore, your mentor should have successfully written the UFE on a repeat attempt. This way you will ensure you have someone to work with you who can relate to your situation as an experienced writer. You also need someone who isn't just going to tell you that everything is going to be okay; you need someone who can walk you through the steps. However, if you pick someone who is not helping you appropriately (who doesn't return your phone calls, or who just doesn't seem to care) then it is your responsibility to take action. This is your UFE summer! You need to have the determination to take charge and find a new mentor if you need to.

UFE Markers

It is also important to have good markers. Dedicated markers are important because they help to make sure that you are on the right track and getting feedback on weaknesses. I suggest one to four markers. If you have more than one marker you will have a few opinions on your writing style and weaknesses and also ensure that you don't swamp one marker, giving you a better chance of getting cases back in a timely manner.

Your markers are not a replacement for your own marking and debriefing. Having a marker should help to ensure that you are accurately marking your own work, by comparing their marking to how you mark yourself, but it doesn't replace marking your own paper. Marking and debriefing is where you learn, so don't sell yourself short. I discuss debriefing in detail on Page 119 in Chapter Three.

At the beginning of the summer you should determine which cases are going to be marked and put them into your study schedule. Let the marker know when to expect your cases so that they can be prepared to mark them in a timely manner for you. Who can be a marker? Anyone! If you are at a Big Four firms ask a successful experienced writer at work, previous UFE writers, and managers who have stayed up-to-date with the UFE. If you don't have these resources at your firm, then hire someone. There are lots of people who mark and mentor each summer for a fee.

To Fire or Not to Fire

CASB (in the Western Provinces) has a document that they release every year that talks about your UFE summer, and it includes a portion on mentors (it is also applicable to markers.) In the document they suggest what you can expect from your mentor and if you don't get what is expected of them, you should fire them. Your mentor is meant to help you pass the UFE and if you aren't getting what you need from them you need to forget about whether you are hurting their feelings and do what is right for you.

In the second summer I was faced with this situation. The firm I worked for provided experienced writers with a marker. Mine was very knowledgeable on the UFE and was considered an expert. I knew him from previous accounting projects, and found him quite nice and helpful, so I thought that he would be a great resource for me. I was wrong.

He was hired by the firm to mark cases for all of the experienced writers at my firm. It was great to get extra feedback, but he didn't mark our cases within an appropriate timeline. It would take a couple of weeks or more to get his comments, at which point I was significantly ahead of where I had been when I had written the case. This made it very discouraging and demotivating because I would be reviewing work I had done weeks before thinking "I should be better than this by now" and of course I was.

In the end I had to fire him. His mentoring style was not appropriate for me. The incident that finally forced my decision was this: I met him at his office one day to review a case I had written four weeks before. This in itself is a red flag because all cases should be marked and returned within a few days. He was fifteen minutes late for the appointment and then he made me wait as he made a ten minute phone call. These actions made it clear to me that I was not a priority. The meeting was in August as my confidence was building. I was determined to pass and I was learning more and more what I needed in order to do that. But at this meeting he told me that I needed to work harder and that I was a candidate for failing if I wasn't careful. He said that my writing style wasn't clear and that I needed to improve significantly. This stressed me out and I left his office upset. Was I really going to fail again? I went for a walk for the next twenty minutes trying to talk myself up again, reminding myself of the confidence I needed to pass the UFE, reminding myself that he was talking about a case I had written four weeks before and that it was no longer relevant to how I was currently doing. But it didn't matter what I said to myself. His words weighed heavily on me. I started having a hard time sleeping due to the high stress and felt like I was falling behind, all because of the comments of one person who was reviewing a case from weeks before.

And then I realized: I was getting good feedback from my other markers and I could see myself improving. The marker hired by the firm was stressing me out based on information that was no longer relevant, so why was I listening to his feedback? Although it was a difficult decision because he had been hired by the firm on my behalf, I sent him an email to let him know not to expect my next case. Sending that email alleviated so much stress and I was able to move on and focus on my studying.

Taking this action required a lot of self-confidence. I had to determine whether he was right that I was behind or whether it was just his way of motivating me. He was trying to motivate me by scaring me, but I didn't need that! I was scared enough after failing once, I didn't need to be scared into studying harder.

This is your summer. Your marker and your mentor are there to help you, and if it isn't working for you then take action!

Helpful Hint: Markers do not have to be experienced writers to provide appropriate feedback, however if they are also providing a mentor-like role I would suggest that you have someone who was also an experienced writer.

A Note on Markers
Big firm versus small firm

I was lucky enough to be working at a Big Four firm in a large metropolitan centre so there were lots of resources available for me to utilize. That is often not the case and many experienced candidates do no have markers and mentors readily available. However, any firm UFE training program that has had long-term success has an effective UFE mentoring system in place and also a culture of anticipated success. UFE mentors can be very effective in helping you achieve UFE success. Unfortunately, there are good mentors and bad mentors. If you are fortunate enough to have a mentor, it is important to ensure your UFE mentor is giving you what you need.

If you are at a small firm without a mentor as a resource, you always have the option of hiring a mentor. If you get a good mentor, it will be well worth your money, as he or she will guide you through the process and help your with every step.

Markers are also available in-house in the larger firms, and there are also markers who mark on a contract basis for candidates who work at small firms who don't provide markers. Many of these people will also provide debriefing and mentoring services if you contract for that. These markers are always in high demand so you want to contact them and arrange something quickly. They also tend to be extremely busy, so it's important to talk about deadlines and turn-around times. If you submit cases late, do not expect a quick turn-around time as they will have moved on to other marking.

 *Deadline: Get a marker and or mentor now. They book up fast!*

Use the following few pages to make notes about markers and mentors. Write down a list of people you might be able to use as a mentor or marker within your firm, or search the internet for someone you can hire.

Markers and mentors:

_____

_____

_____

_____

_____

_____

_____

_____

_____

_____

_____

_____

_____

Markers and mentors (Cont.):

CHAPTER TWO SUMMARY

You've had your time to feel sorry for yourself, but now it's time to get determined. Get organized! Plan your summer! Talk to successful experienced writers! I have provided a checklist below so you don't forget anything.

February Checklist:

1. Re-read Chapter Two of "I Failed the UFE! Now What? A survival guide."
2. Create the study schedule that will work for you. Check out the Appendix on Page 219 for a sample study plan.
3. Make sure you are signed up for a July course. If you're not in a course, then you should get on a waitlist!
4. Become determined!
5. Interview successful experienced writers. Make a list of questions and take them for coffee.
6. Find a study partner.
7. Find a mentor.
8. Find marking support.

Have other action items for February? Use the following pages to write them down:

February action items (Cont.):

"Success is always temporary. When all is said and done, the only thing you'll have left is your character."
- Vince Gill -
Musician

CHAPTER TWO QUIZ: ARE YOU BACK ON THE HORSE?
... or still scared to ride?

Read the following questions and answer as honestly as possible on a scale of 1 to 5. (1 = Never 5 = Always)

1. I know that I shouldn't start studying now. I promise not to study until it's time!

   1   2   3   4   5

2. I have a plan of action and I feel confident I know what to do to make sure I'm ready for the summer.

   1   2   3   4   5

3. I have a study plan and a study partner.

   1   2   3   4   5

4. I have researched what course to take, and I have signed up (or, on the waitlist) for my desired course.

   1   2   3   4   5

5. I have interviewed several experienced writers (or, I have interviews set up.) The more the better.

   1   2   3   4   5

6. I know that I can pass the UFE and I am determined to win the game.

   1   2   3   4   5

7. I have looked around my neighbourhood and have found the perfect study location.

   1   2   3   4   5

8. I have a mentor and a marker. They are dedicated to me passing the UFE.
           1   2   3   4   5

9. I know the flow-through rate for UFE writers is almost 100%, and that gives me the confidence to know that I can do this!
           1   2   3   4   5

10. I am motivated. I am confident. This is my year!
            1   2   3   4   5

NOW ADD UP YOUR POINTS AND SEE WHERE YOU FIT IN BELOW.

If your score is between 10 and 24 points: *You're getting back on the horse in a big way!*

Being organized and prepared before you start studying is a great way to keep your nerves at bay as the study season approaches. You are organized and have a plan of action, which is the perfect way to make sure you start off on the right foot! And now you can relax. There's no studying to do yet. All you have to do is stay motivated, confident, and positive!

If your score is between 25 and 39 points: *You're working on the logistics and you're going to be back on the horse in no time!*

You are doing your best to get organized so that you are ready when the study season starts, and that's fabulous. Make sure you keep working on it so that you don't find yourself in July with no mentor and no study partner. But at the same time, it's nothing to stress about. If you are this far already, you'll keep moving forward and be ready by the time July is here. Remember to stay motivated, confident, and positive.

If your score is between 40 and 50 points: *You're having a hard time getting started.*

You don't know where to start. It's all so overwhelming! There is a lot to think about and do, not to mention the full swing of busy season and the emotions that failing the UFE has imposed. But don't get discouraged. You still have several months until studying begins. Baby steps. Read below and determine which one of the three listed most closely resembles your situation, and take action!

Your exercise: You need to find out what is keeping you from getting your UFE summer organized. Here are some ideas of what might be holding you back:

1. **My work schedule is crazy busy!** If you're busy with work and that's

what's keeping you from getting organized, that's okay. Don't let it get you down. There will come a time in the not-so- distant future when work will give you an evening to yourself (although I know that's hard to believe) and you will have time to sit down and start getting organized. Don't stress about it. You'll find time. And for now, ask around at work in order to start the process of finding a study-buddy, a mentor and some markers.

2. **I'm not sure where to start!** That's understandable. There certainly is a lot to think about, so start small. Ask a successful experienced writer if you can interview them. It might seem hard at first, but after doing one you'll see that everyone truly wants to help you succeed at the UFE. Have questions ready so that you don't forget what you want to ask them if you get nervous. Another good place to start is researching deadlines for signing up for things. Once you get a picture of when the deadlines are, you'll have a better grasp on what you need to do to get signed up and ready to roll! Try doing one or two things every week, that way it won't feel as overwhelming.

3. **It's just too early to start thinking about all this stuff!** You're right, it is early. There's no harm in waiting for a little while, but what's the point in leaving it until the last minute so that you are scrambling at the end of June to find a study partner, a study location, a mentor, and markers? Write out a study schedule; sign up for courses (which, if you wait, will be full by July anyway) and the UFE. It's better to start now and do as much as you can before the study summer starts so that when the time comes there is no additional stress. Get started now!

Have your own ideas about how you are feeling? Use the following pages to write them down, along with what you can do to take action!

February - ideas, feelings, actions:

February - ideas, feelings, actions (Cont.):

February - ideas, feelings, actions (Cont.):

> "Every worth while accomplishment, big or little, has its stages of drudgery and triumph; a beginning, a struggle and a victory."
> - Mahatma Ghandi -
> Political and spiritual leader of India

CHAPTER THREE: MARCH THROUGH JULY
And the studying begins!

Studying This Year

This chapter begins in March. This is because you will want to start getting organized in the spring as busy season at work slows down. You will write a few questions to get comfortable with writing cases again, do some technical review to bring you back up to speed, and become confident that this is your year. Although getting organized and comfortable with cases again begins in March, full time study does not! Study smarter, not more! See the Appendix on Page 219 for the suggested study plan.

The Traditional Study Schedule

Use the eight week period in March and April to write, have marked, and debrief three non-comp simulations. This is busy season so the objective is to keep the UFE work in any one week reasonable. A simulation should be written one week, sent for marking or marked yourself and then debriefed the next week. There are eight weeks and only three simulations (see the Appendix on Page 219 for a sample study schedule.) This reflects the reality that there will be some weeks that you are just so crazy busy that realistically you are not going to do any studying.

Helpful Hint: Studying this year is going to be unlike your first year in many ways because you have done this before and can use your knowledge as leverage. Learn from your mistakes in the first summer and reinvent your study schedule. Have your list of weaknesses in front of you while you study so that you can work on them every day and they can become your strengths (see Page 43 in Chapter One.) If you didn't like where you studied last summer, then change the location. If you remember being really tired on Fridays then use your flex day as a light study afternoon. If you remember pushing through study days when you felt burnt out, then learn from that mistake; allow yourself some days off when you feel overworked.

Remember: *Over the course of the summer you will be doing at least four years worth of UFE questions, so taking an afternoon off and missing one case because you are burnt out won't mean you'll fail the UFE. It is a good investment to make sure that you stay rested and focused. Don't study more. Study smarter.*

Study Partners
Revisited

I talked a lot about study partners in Chapter Two. The following studying discussion should be linked to your study partner decision because you need to make sure that you are studying with a person who is on the same schedule as you. You don't want to study with someone who doesn't want to do Friday Flex days, or who might guilt trip you if you take an afternoon off when you are burnt out. You need to do what works for you and you need a study partner who is okay with that, and who wants a similar study schedule.

It's Like Running a Marathon
Baby steps

Studying will be more familiar to you now than in the first summer, but don't be fooled. This does not mean that it will be easy. When you write your first simulation in the spring you might be surprised at how hard it is and how much you have forgotten since the UFE last September. I remember writing my first simulation and being so disorganized and confused; I didn't even remember how to find the issues!

I am a runner, and I like to compare rewriting the UFE to running a marathon. When I train for a marathon I run a lot every day for months. Week after week I slowly work up to running the length of a marathon, and then I run a marathon. But If I wanted to run a marathon a year later I wouldn't be able to just go out and run it because a year ago I had trained really hard to be able to run a marathon. I would have to train for a marathon again, starting right back at the beginning. That first run would be really hard but as time went on I would work back up to my marathon stamina and be able to run another marathon even better than the first.

The same is true for studying for the UFE. Don't be surprised if you bomb your first case or even your first several cases. You haven't reviewed technical, how to outline, or the structure of the case writing in several months so it is expected that you don't remember how to do it. And if you do, well that's amazing! You are ahead of where I was so that should improve your confidence in knowing you can pass.

"I Am an Experienced Writer"
Say it with confidence

I couldn't stand the embarrassment of saying "I am an experienced writer." It made me cringe inside. Most people at the firm knew that I had failed, my friends who had written the UFE and passed knew I had failed, and my friends and family knew I had failed. But it was still hard for me to say it out loud. I simply couldn't say "I failed the UFE."

The firm that I was working for had a UFE course that included several days scattered throughout the spring and a full week in July. There were four experienced writers. It was a relief that I wasn't the only one because in a room full of sixty people it was hard enough being one of four, but if I had been alone it would have been much worse.

The first session of the program was held in a hotel in downtown Vancouver. Walking through the doors the first day was hard. My heart was racing and my pride was more than a little bruised. Some people probably didn't know that I was an experienced writer, but it felt like everyone knew!

This was that same day that I had a moment of realization that changed the course of the summer for me. I wouldn't call it an epiphany exactly, (that's a bit strong) but it was something like that. I realized that I wasn't going to have enough confidence to pass the UFE if I continued to hide and feel embarrassed about studying. The reality was that I had failed the UFE and I needed to rewrite it. If I couldn't say that out loud, how was I ever going to be able to accept it and pass? Therefore, I forced myself to start saying it. I was committed to saying it without cringing, and to fight off the feeling of embarrassment. At first it was hard but as I worked up to saying it more often it was so liberating! It was freeing to say "I am an experienced writer" without feeling sorry for myself. It was a fact, and I treated it as such instead of taking on the emotions of it.

I started small by saying it in my head. When this got easy, I started saying it to other people. I noticed that nobody else would bring the subject up with me, so I started saying it and it became a less fragile topic. First-time writers started asking me for advice, what studying was like, what the UFE was like, and what to expect. It was empowering to accept it and embrace it, much more so than pretending it had never happened. Saying it out loud allowed me to accept it and gain confidence, and it allowed me to be a resource to other writers by talking about my experiences.

Helpful Hint: In order to pass the UFE you need to have confidence that you can pass it, and to have confidence you need to be comfortable saying that you failed last year!

If you can't accept that you are an experienced writer then how can you really feel confident that you will pass the UFE this year? You can't! You need to accept that you have to write it again and move on, and this doesn't mean just thinking that you have accepted it. It means truly accepting it. Don't fool yourself into thinking you have accepted it and just move on by saying that talking about it just isn't for you. Some people find it difficult to accept that emotions have anything to do with the UFE and try to cover up their emotions. This is a temporary fix to a bigger problem. If you just cover up the fact that you are cringing at the thought of being an experienced writer, you will have a very difficult time studying this summer and being confident in your abilities to pass.

This is your year to pass! Resolve yourself to do everything in your power to pass. Start small. Start saying in your head right now "I am an experienced writer." How does that make you feel? Does it make you cringe? If it does, try saying it again but this time clear your mind, sit up straight and put a smile on your face. Now say: "I am an experienced writer." Say it as many times as you need to in order to feel confident that you will be able to say it to someone else out loud. When this feels okay, add onto it to make it a positive statement, i.e. an affirmation: "I am an experienced writer. I am ahead of the game because I have been through all of this before and I know what to expect. I am confident that I will pass."

It sounds corny and cheesy I know, and it might feel a bit weird at first, but you don't have to have anyone else around. This is all about you. Say it in the privacy of your home, say it while you're running, biking, or wherever you have to be to feel alone enough that you can say it first in your head and then out loud. I swear it worked for me, and what's the harm in trying it out to see if it works for you too? Give it a try! And once you have that down and it feels okay saying it to yourself, I challenge you to openly say it to other people. If they don't know you are an experienced writer, don't pretend that you aren't. Be honest. Accepting that you are an experienced writer allows you to remind yourself that it isn't a bad thing that you have to write again. It's certainly inconvenient, but it isn't something that should make you feel like you are lesser than those people who pass the first time. You are just as good as the first-time writers, and being honest with yourself and everyone else will drastically improve your confidence. "I am an experienced writer and this is my year!" Say it with confidence and conviction.

Psychologist
Someone neutral to talk to

Going to a psychologist means that you are willing to accept that you can't do everything on your own and you want help working through a difficult time in your life. Failing the UFE constitutes a difficult time in your life. The support from your wife, husband, partner, girlfriend, boyfriend, fiancé, mother, father, sister, brother, best friend etc. is fabulous, and cannot be underestimated. We cannot do this without them! But sometimes some of us need to talk to someone who doesn't have anything invested in us and who can give an unbiased view. Now granted, not all experienced writers will need this, but for those of us who do need help, a psychologist can be invaluable.

When I decided to go to a sports psychologist it was embarrassing at first. I didn't feel comfortable and I didn't know what to say. But I really found it helpful to talk to someone who didn't know anything about me, or the UFE but would listen to me talk about the UFE with a perspective of increasing my performance and winning.

The UFE is very much like high level competitive sports. A sports psychologist is a great way to learn how to visualize triumph, but talking to anyone who is able to teach you how to decrease stress is valuable.

Helpful Hint: Some firms have confidential stress counseling as part of their employee benefits package. Some provincial institutes provide stress counseling for those members and students, not covered by employer plans, who are experiencing negative stress effects. Generally those services are provided free of charge but should only be used appropriately by those candidates experiencing severe stress.

Stress
Anxiety that's motivating

Sports psychologists aren't just for athletes. Whether you're an athlete or a UFE writer, the idea is the same: you want to be able to visualize winning. If seeing the word "sports" in the title frightens you, know this: it's not an exclusive club for athletes. Seeing a sports psychologist can be very beneficial to UFE writers too.

I have said it before and I will say it again. The UFE is stressful. UFE related stress is one of the main reasons that many people, myself included, fail the UFE. Why is it so stressful? Because from the time we get started on the path towards becoming a Chartered Accountant there is an exam we hear about that has to be completed before we get those coveted letters behind our name. People love to scare us. "So many people fail" (we hear). "It is almost insurmountable" (we hear). But it's not true!

I spoke to one woman who was writing the UFE for the third time when I was rewriting (she passed!) She was an honours student in University and had never failed a test. The UFE was different for her, she said, not because of the content but because of the mystique around it. From the very moment that her first manager at work told her that it was the hardest test she would ever take and that even the smartest people fail, she was extremely nervous and suffered from high anxiety over the UFE. That was the beginning of her extreme UFE challenge. To get over the mystique of the UFE took her three attempts, but she was an honours student and a brilliant woman so there was no reason she shouldn't have passed on her first try. Except for the stress.

It is extremely important to know when your stress is mounting and to confront it. In my first year I thought I was dealing with my stress, but I wasn't. My way of dealing with it was to know that it was there, accept it, and continue to feel stressed. Here was my problem: I thought that if I didn't have high anxiety about the UFE that I wasn't taking it seriously. I sometimes noticed myself purposely increasing my anxiety because I felt like that meant I was taking it seriously.

In my second year I went to see a Sports Psychologist. Going to see a psychologist is surprisingly hard on the ego. Why is that? Some people see it as a weakness when we need help with something, but the fact is that knowing what you need is an important strength. Helping yourself and becoming a stronger and better person is what we all strive for in life, so we shouldn't be afraid to ask for help sometimes. In Chapter Two I say that there are four main reasons that I passed the UFE, one of which was seeing a sports psychologist. She was instrumental in helping me learn how to effectively deal with anxiety, which ultimately led to my success on the UFE.

She explained to me that anxiety is motivating to a certain level, however once it gets over a certain threshold it is de-motivating. An example of motivating anxiety is when an athlete has butterflies in her stomach. This small amount of anxiety is motivating. It helps the athlete get focused and excited about the competition and get off to a strong start. An example of de-motivating anxiety is when an athlete is so nervous that she becomes sick, has low energy and is unable to perform to her full potential. Clearly in this situation the anxiety has become so severe that it is de-motivating.

My husband, Todd, is a stand-up comedian (if you need a laugh go to **www.ToddAllen.ca.** Shameless promotion of my favourite comedian!) He has been performing comedy for eleven years so his experience gives him confidence and limits his anxiety when he goes on stage. For a typical show he has just enough anxiety that he has butterflies, which makes it exciting for him to perform. However, when I have gone to watch his shows I have also watched new comedians perform. For them it is a much different experience, and provides a good example of demotivating anxiety. A new comedian who has had significantly less stage time than Todd has higher anxiety and less confidence. I have seen many new comedians pacing in the green room, reading and re-reading their material and suffering from sweaty palms. When they finally get in front of the audience they are less likely to be able to ad lib when the show changes directions unexpectedly (usually thanks to a drunk audience member) and thus are less likely to perform to their full potential.

As you can see from the athlete and comedian examples, there is a certain amount of motivating anxiety but once anxiety increases beyond a certain level, it has a negative impact and is de-motivating.

It is important to learn how to keep your anxiety at a level that is motivating. Learning how to control your anxiety and keep it motivating, without reaching the threshold of de-motivating, is going to be very useful. The more anxiety you feel while writing the UFE, the less likely you will be able to concentrate and do well. The three days of the UFE is a test of your abilities to work under stressful conditions and come out on top. It's exhausting and if you do not know how to keep your anxiety at a motivating level it can be disastrous.

In the book "Blink" Malcolm Gladwell describes what he calls "temporary autism" where people get into a highly stressful situation and are not able to act as they normally would. He tells a story about a black man named Amadou Diallo who lived in the South Bronx after having recently moved from Guinea. One night in February 1999 just after midnight, he stood outside of his apartment looking around his neighbourhood. Because it was a poor neighbourhood with rampant drug trade, he looked suspicious to four plain clothed officers patrolling the streets that night. As the officers approached, Diallo became so afraid he started to run, knowing that a man had been robbed in his neighbourhood days before. The fact that he was running and pulling something out of his pocket as he did so, made the officers anxious and they shot and killed him, later finding only a wallet in his hand where they expected a gun.

Gladwell argues that the officers had temporary autism. An autistic person, as he explains it, has difficulty interpreting nonverbal cues, such as gestures and facial expressions, or putting themselves inside someone else's head. They are "mind-blind" i.e. they do not have the ability to read a person's expressions and link the expressions to the situation. On the UFE I think we would call "mind blind" the "big picture." If you are autistic, you are unable to see the big picture.

That night in the South Bronx when the plain clothes officers shot Diallo they were not seeing the big picture. They had temporary autism. They thought Diallo looked suspicious standing there alone at night in a bad neighbourhood. The truth was that he had just arrived home and was enjoying the evening air. They thought Diallo was running from the cops. He thought they were robbing him. They thought that Diallo had a gun. He had a wallet.

Gladwell goes on to explain that your heart beat has to be in a certain range for optimal stress. The optimal state of stress, where stress improves performance, is between 115 and 145 Beats Per Minute. When it goes beyond this, bad things start to happen because there is a breakdown of cognitive processing. Therefore, performing in high stress situations that are beyond optimal is almost impossible...unless you train yourself to do it. Gladwell believes that if the plain clothed officers had had more experience they would have been able to react differently. They were new to the Street Crime Unit, but with training they would have been able to gather more information, or see the big picture, and come to the right conclusion: that Diallo was not a criminal and that all he had was a wallet. Studies and training programs have shown that if you train yourself to do something under a high stress situation you will be able to perform better, i.e. you will be able to remain within your optimal range. For example, there have been many situations when someone in an emergency picks up the phone and dials 411 instead of 911, because the situation is so stressful and they have never practiced dialing 911.

Now let's link all of this back to the UFE. I think it is fair to say that writing the UFE is not as stressful as shooting a man, or an emergency where you are required to dial 911. But what I am illustrating to you is that being able to perform under stress at your optimal level is absolutely essential and it takes practice. You have to train yourself to write

UFE questions and decrease your stress so that all three days of the UFE you stay in your optimal range and can write the cases and see the big picture. If you are so stressed that you have a case of temporary autism (although an actual case of temporary autism is unlikely, as it is linked to extreme stress situations), then something bad will happen. You will not be in your optimal range. You will not be able to see the big picture. And you will not be able to pass the UFE.

Learn How to Deal With Your Stress
So that it's second nature during the UFE

Based on the above discussion, learning to deal with your anxiety now will ensure that you will perform well on the UFE when stress is high, you're tired, and something that isn't familiar comes up on Day Three. If you are someone who experiences high stress, a sports psychologist is something you should consider. I do not take lightly the impact it had on me for my second UFE summer. After two sessions with a sports psychologist I was given the tools I needed to handle my stress and use my anxiety to my advantage. In other words, I learned how to be in my optimal stress range. This, along with dedicating myself to my study schedule and debriefing well every day, made it possible for me to perform in my optimal range on all three days of the UFE. And that's why I passed.

Anxiety
Decreasing anxiety to take control of stress

I have provided a very simple but effective exercise for decreasing anxiety. It's similar to the one on being positive that I talk about in Chapter One on Page 38, but this one has you experiencing how you will feel upon passing the UFE by visualizing the feeling of passing.

In this exercise you are talking in the future, about the past. You are talking about passing the UFE (which is in the future) as though it's in the past (i.e. as though now it's January of next year, for example, and passing the UFE has already happened.) You are going to create what are called affirmations that you can say to yourself when you feel high anxiety. Say each one as you breathe in for five seconds and out for three seconds.

Below are some examples of the ones that I used:
1. It feels so good to know that I passed the UFE!
2. It feels so good to know that next summer I don't have to study for the UFE!
3. It feels so good to have my CA!

A note about "affirmations": I think this word can sound flaky to some people because of its connection to New Age thought. But try to think of it as what it is, affirming your belief in something, which in our case is essentially positive thinking. There's nothing wrong with that, right?

Keep your Anxiety at a Motivating Level

I would say these affirmations to myself whenever I felt the rise of anxiety: as I was lying awake in bed at night, riding my bike, making dinner, or hanging out with friends. I used this exercise and noticed an amazing transformation; the ability to keep my anxiety at a motivating level. By saying these affirmations to myself I started to actually believe them. My anxiety started to decrease and I started sleeping through the night and enjoying my weekends and evenings more. I had less anxiety and more motivation, and I knew now that I could pass the UFE.

Write down your affirmations here and reflect back on them often. Earmark the page so they're easy to find!

_____

_____

_____

_____

_____

_____

Affirmations (Cont.):

Relaxation and Vacations
Having a balanced summer

Balancing your summer by having a little fun is simply necessary, and why wouldn't you want to? When is the next time you're going to get off early every day during the summer? It's going to be awhile, so take advantage of it while you can.

My second UFE summer was my best summer in years because I got off early every day allowing me a lot of time to do what I like to do. I trained for a triathlon, spent a lot of time at the beach, and had lots of time to hang out with friends and family. Having all of this freedom and fun made it a lot easier to stay centered and focused on the UFE when I was studying, without getting too stressed. The second summer was better than my first summer because I really learned how to deal with my anxiety and stay relaxed.

I recommend that you write fun adventures into your schedule to make it balanced. I talked to one experienced writer who told me that she considered her second summer her "Summer of Fun." She always had something entertaining planned for the weekend, like going away on a shopping trip with a girlfriend, meeting friends for dinner, or going camping. And she took long weekends off. This helped her to stay focused when she was at the library studying, because she was relaxed when she wasn't at the library. I followed her advice and it worked.

I took one week off in the middle of studying. It allowed me to study for a couple of weeks and have a week off to look forward to. It also motivated me to work harder and feel really good about my progress so that when I went on the week vacation, I wasn't stressed that I should be studying. I also took long weekends off and I would always take the Friday off if I had a friend or family coming in for the weekend. Taking a week off and having long weekends scattered into my summer was a very important part of my balanced study schedule. It helped me to relax when I wasn't in the library, and work hard when I was. I was motivated when I was studying because I always had something to look forward to.

Bruce Densmore explains in 'UFE Success' that when he studied for the UFE he was studying day and night all summer, watching his results decrease the more he studied.

With a stroke of luck he ran into a colleague who offered advice on a more balanced study approach. Bruce went on to pass the UFE, but without a balanced study plan he admits he doesn't know if he would have.

Along with scheduled days off, be cognizant of how you are feeling. If you feel like you are starting to burn out, you should consider taking an afternoon off. I did this on two occasions and I returned the next day refreshed and re-motivated. See my explanation on burnout on Page 114. Make sure you know what it feels like because taking a day off for burnout is an important part of a relaxed and balanced study schedule. Many experienced writers take a UFE course in mid to late July and then start their serious four weeks of study in mid August. There is a period between the training course and serious study that is perfect if you want to take a mini vacation.

Remember: Nobody can pass this exam without studying, but you have to study smart. Having a balanced summer and not burning out is part of a smart study schedule. You will be doing a significant number of cases over the course of the summer, so taking long weekends off or an afternoon for burnout won't cause you to fail the UFE. You have to be serious about your study but also have fun this summer!

Burnout
What it feels like and how to avoid it

Burnout is when you are exhausted and unable to function as you normally would. When I am burnt out I often don't realize it until after I have recuperated, so it is a bit tricky to learn what it feels like. But if you are typically good at staying focused and doing your work and one day you notice that you are having a hard time focusing and writing cases, then chances are you are experiencing burn out, and should take a break. When you are burnt out it feels like you don't care anymore. 'Who cares if I fail the UFE' or 'Who cares if I don't study anymore.' You basically lose all motivation to do work.

I think it is safe to say that if you have worked in a public accounting firm, you have felt burnt out before! If you have gotten this far in becoming an accountant then you have done well in university, have been through more than one busy season at an accounting firm, and have done all of the necessary pre-requisites to the UFE. Suffice to say that your life has been full of accomplishment, not all of which came without stress.

It is quite likely that you have experienced burnout during busy season. You work extremely long hours on at least one job, often several at a time, trying to get in sleep and maybe even some exercise, while still trying to live your own life. Being able to pull that off doesn't come without a little bit of stress. However, you may not even realize that you are burnt out! It's an easy thing to push aside because you have been working hard for years to get to this point, and you've pushed through it before.

But it's not a good idea to push through it for the UFE. Pushing through burnout makes it difficult for your brain to function, so a three day exam with intricate detail, technical requirements, and big picture thought is impossible to accomplish if you're burnt out. So make sure you study smart. Know what it feels like when you get burnt out. Take my advice about relaxing so that you can have a balanced summer and reduce your potential for burnout. And if you feel burnout coming on, take time off immediately to rejuvenate. Take the afternoon off and do something fun, whether it's a game of golf or dinner with friends. A distraction will put you on the right track to be refreshed for studying the next day.

Sleep
Get some zzzzzz's

I am not a good sleeper and it gets worse when I'm stressed, so when I rewrote the UFE I wanted to learn how to sleep better. So I started experimenting. When I woke up in the middle of the night and couldn't go back to sleep, I would do the anxiety exercise in my head (see Page 111). I would repeat my affirmations over and over again, visualizing each one and how each accomplishment would make me feel. And it worked. Success!

If this doesn't work for you, there are other solutions: books on sleep, valerian tea, serotonin, and earplugs to name a few. If you are still unable to sleep through the night you can take a mild sleeping pill, but this should be a last resort!

***H**elpful Hint: If you decide you need to take a sleeping pill, make sure you test any it during the summer and not just during the UFE so that you know how it affects you. Some sleeping pills are quite strong, and can make you feel groggy the next day. That is not going to help your UFE performance.*

Outlining

Having a strong outline is crucial. In my opinion, outlining was vital to my success on the UFE when it was unexpectedly undirected in 2008; my outlining skills helped me stay organized.

Everyone has different outlining styles, and if it works for you that's all that matters. But make sure it really does work for you. Do you actually use your outline? I often talk to students who outline, but never use it. Or they start the summer outlining, but then stop half way through the summer. I know a woman who would prepare an outline but she also made a lot of margin notes. Because her information was strewn all over her outline and her margins, she didn't use any of it, which left her disorganized and unable to structure a successful response. Unfortunately she did not pass the UFE.

If you are not outlining, why is this? Is it because it works for you, or because you never have before? It is easy to get used to your status quo of writing cases, but this summer is not about status quo. This summer is about rising above, learning to change, and passing the UFE. If you aren't outlining, then start now so that you have a strong outlining approach by September.

With the use of computers on the UFE the new trend is to do outlining on the computer. I strongly advise against this. I tried it myself because I had this idea that it would be faster because I would already have all the information on the computer. It seemed ingenious! But what I discovered was that I spent so much time scrolling up and down to look at it, that my responses were suffering. Time is crucial on the UFE, and I was wasting it by scrolling up and down. I tried another approach: I would insert my discussion into the outline that I made on the computer, so that I didn't have to scroll up and down as much, and all the information from within my outline became my response. This resulted in poor responses because I was so busy fitting things into the outline and expanding on thoughts, that my writing style became weak. It also made it more difficult for me to see the "Big Picture" and hit the Pervasive indicators.

If you are outlining on your computer, why is this? Do you ever look at it or does it take too much time to scroll up and down so you don't bother? Does it affect the quality of your response by (a) taking too much time, (b) not referring to it, or (c) negatively affecting your writing style? Does it seem inefficient? I suggest that you try doing your outline on a piece of paper and see whether you use it more (try it more than once!) I suspect your response will be stronger and more structured.

On my website (www.KaylaSwitzer.com) there is an example of outlining. This is the outlining approach I used the second time I wrote and it was very effective. Try it out, and change it as required to match your style!

Outlining Steps
Follow these steps every time!

See the example on my website at www.KaylaSwitzer.com

1. If the short text is a full page or longer, read the last one or two paragraphs of the front page and pick out the requireds. Write them down word-for-word (otherwise you might change the meaning slightly, which can be devastating to your response). If the short text is a half to two thirds of a page then it may be a better strategy to just start reading from the top of the text to find the real required and then reread all of the text again.

2. Read the remaining first page of the case, inserting the following at the top of your outline: date ('Now' and/or a timeline), role, and users. Write down any additional requireds you might find (if necessary), and reread all of the requireds to ensure you have copied them down correctly.

3. Read the remaining case. Insert information under the required it relates to. Reference the information between the outline and the case as much as possible in order to keep the amount of information on your outline simple (i.e. number the paragraph it comes from, and put the number on your outline with a quick note about what the paragraph is about. You shouldn't rewrite the case on your outline!) Make it easy to reference back to where it is in in the case. If there are additional real requireds in the exhibits then add them to your outline.

4. Review your outline. Write what competency area you think each required is, if they are primary or secondary, which indicators integrate, the big picture, ranking and time allocations. This is all part of the strategic thinking process. Write all of this clearly on your outline in a different colour if necessary, so that it stands out.

5. Refer to your outline as you write your response.

Helpful Hint: If the case is undirected with several requireds within the exhibits, it's hard to know while you're reading which indicator certain issues relate to. This means that you will need more time to review your outline before you start writing so you can move information around to ensure that all the case facts are under the right requireds.

Remember: Time allocations and ranking are <u>crucial</u> to a strong response. Don't steal time from one indicator for another, because if you get Highly Competent on an indicator and Nominally Competent on another, what's the point? If you always do really well on one or two indicators and don't score on the others, you can't pass Level One, Breadth. Additionally, if you aren't ranking, i.e. talking about the most important or time critical issues, you will not be able to get depth. Rank and stay on time for every case.

Debriefing
The most important part of studying!

I cannot stress enough the importance of debriefing. Debriefing is where you learn your technical, how to get depth, the triggers, and a concise writing style. In short it's where you learn *everything*. You need to debrief well so that you can get the most out of it, and to do this (as with your outline) you need an approach.

Debriefing cannot start until there is a marked response. I marked my own responses and backed this up once or twice a week with the use of external markers from my firm to validate my marking results. Like I discussed on Page 86, you may not have markers in you firm. However, markers can be hired and should be hired if you have no other option.) Once you have marked your response, it's time to debrief. Below is the approach I used for debriefing. I recommend you use it every time you debrief to make sure that you are marking and debriefing efficiently and effectively every time.

How to Debrief
Follow this every single time you write a case

Debriefing your case is absolutely, without a doubt, the most important part of studying. If you don't debrief your case in detail there is no point in ever writing it. When you debrief, you learn what you are doing right, so you can keep doing it right, and what you are doing wrong and need to improve on. You learn what technical you don't know, and then you review and learn that technical. You learn how to refine your outline so it's working for you. Essentially, everything about writing a strong case comes from debriefing each case in detail and learning from it.

At first debriefing will take a long time, maybe longer than twice what it takes to write the case. But as the summer progresses you will start getting a lot faster at debriefing because you will be doing better on your cases and will know more technical, so debriefing might take less than twice what it takes to write the case by September.

Debriefing is NOT reading the evaluation guide. You will not learn anything from simply reading the guide. Debriefing IS following every single step of the approach below, every single time. And if technical is the issue, then review your technical right then and there during the debrief. Too often I hear of students who fail the UFE because when they debriefed a question they would make a list of technical that they needed to review "later", and by September that list was so long that they didn't have time to learn it all, freaked out, lost confidence, didn't learn their technical, and failed the UFE. Don't let this happen to you!

Debriefing Steps

1. Compare your outline to the solution:
- Did you miss indicators? Why? What was the trigger?
- If you didn't get all the issues in an indicator determine why. What's the trigger?

Helpful Hint: Know the trigger! The trigger is what leads you to knowing that there is an issue to talk about in the case. Knowing the trigger is so important, because you will start to see patterns where certain triggers mean that there are certain issues. After writing a couple weeks worth of cases, you will notice triggers repeating themselves.

2. Consider time budget for each indicator:
- How much time did you give yourself? Is the time budget reasonable? If not, how would you allot time for the same issues next time?
- Did you stick to the time budgets? If not, was it because your allocation was unreasonable? Or was it because you didn't limit yourself to the allotted time? How can you improve next time?

Helpful Hint: Get a timer that counts down! For each case, set the time allotted, and use it to track the time spent on reading, outlining, and writing each indicator. *This will make it so much easier than using the clock on your computer. Just make sure it's a silent timer so your alarm doesn't go off during the UFE!*

Remember: *Poor time management often results in a failed attempt on the UFE. Don't steal time from one indicator to do well on another. This leads to a failed attempt at Level I because you are not able to hit enough indicators, i.e. you don't get breadth. Learn how to manage your time within a case!*

    3. **Did you play the correct role?**
- If not, what effect did it have on your response? What is the trigger to know the role next time?

Remember: *Sometimes role doesn't seem like a big deal. But be careful, because in some cases if you play the wrong role you don't address the issues correctly and you can't get Competent.*

    4. **Consider ranking:**
- Did you properly rank and discuss major issues. If not, what is the trigger?
- Did you rank within the indicator? If not, how would you rank next time?

Helpful Hint: *Ranking the indicator to talk about first and for how long is important, but just as important is ranking the issues within the indicator to talk about. First you rank the indicators in the order you want to talk about them. Then, within Performance Measurement for example, there will be several possible issues to discuss, so which ones are you going to talk about? It's tempting to talk about all of them, but it's impossible to do this and get depth. Or you might want to talk about the* one you know the best, but you can't do this and get depth either. You need to rank the issues in order of importance, just like you do the indicators, and talk about the biggest, most important, time sensitive issues. You can't talk about all of the issues, and you won't be able to reach Competent talking only about the little accounting issues, so always rank the issues based on relevance to the client.

5. Did you get depth? If not is it because of:

- A Technical Deficiency? If so, then learn the technical!
- A Process problem? Did you know the issue but you weren't quite sure how to address it? Then learn what you need to do to address it next time.
- A Case Writing issue? Is it unclear? Did you think you were talking about the issue, but it didn't come out right? If so, consider a rewrite.

A note on rewrites: Rewriting will help you improve your writing style and will help in your overall case writing skills. To perform your rewrite use your response, but delete everything that isn't necessary. Then, add everything you would write next time (more efficiently of course) in order to get to Competent. Rewriting should only be done early in the study process while you are trying to refine your writing style.

Remember: Don't leave technical until the next day, or the end of the week. Your entire debrief should be done after writing the case, including learning any technical that you didn't know. This means the debriefs in the early part of the summer will take a bit longer, but that's okay. You need to learn the technical, so take the time to learn it all <u>now</u>. If you leave it until the end of the week, you aren't going to have time to review all of it and all of your weaknesses that came up during the week. Too often I am told by students that the reason they failed is that they kept putting off technical study, and then at the end of the summer they had so much to learn that they weren't able to get through it all, and didn't know enough technical to pass the UFE. Don't let this be you! Always complete your debrief before moving on to the next case.

6. Getting to the next level:

- Why did you get Reaching Competent? What prevented you from getting to

Competent? or why did you get Nominally Competent instead of Reaching Competent? Identify the cause of the problem (knowledge, poor time management, missing required pieces, writing issues, not understanding what was required for depth, etc.) then determine how you would score a Competent rating the next time.
- Consider how to apply what you missed to your next case and then write it on a post-it. Stick that note by your desk or put it into your debrief notes, or whatever it takes to remember for next time.

7. Review your outline:
- Is your outline clear? If not, consider why. Does it have too much info? If it does, cross out everything you don't need, in order to show yourself how much less you can have on it next time.
- Is it too sparse? If so consider what needed to be added to make this a useable outline.

8. Did you consider integration on your outline and rank accordingly?
- If you didn't integrate but should have, discover what the trigger is so you can integrate next time. Often indicators need to be considered together. Not all the indicators should be considered completely independently of each other. For example, addressing Assurance and Performance Measurement together is a great way to integrate.

Module 6 and the Simulated UFE
Western provinces only

I did not take Module 6 in my second summer, as I discuss in Chapter Two on Page 71. However, some experienced writers do and that is a choice that you have to make on your own. If you have decided to take Module 6 again, be prepared that it is going to be a different experience compared to your first year. The course itself will be the same, but you are ahead of where the rest of the students are. You have a lot more experience with the UFE and you need to use this to your advantage. Don't just go with the flow and follow along with the class. Make it right for you. For example, in Module 6 they do a lot of cases and sometimes it is hard to have enough time to debrief each one because so much is crammed into each day. But you know the importance of a good debrief, and you've had a lot of experience writing cases, so it might make more sense to write fewer cases and take the time to debrief in more detail. Or, if you want to write all the cases, step outside and debrief on your own while the class is discussing how the UFE is marked, or other information that you already know about the UFE.

During Module 6 you will write several cases that are marked by external markers. This is a great way to get some feedback and compare it to how you are marking yourself. However, be careful here. Don't let your confidence waiver if you are not doing as well as you feel you should be doing because these cases are much different than UFE cases. CASB cases are not representative of UFE cases.

Remember: Module 6 cases are not representative of the UFE. They are much more technical and specific in what is required to achieve Competent and this makes it more difficult to hit indicators. Accept the comments from the markers, and improve using any suggestions, but remember that past UFE cases are more representative.

CHAPTER THREE SUMMARY

March through July is a busy time. You will study some technical, start writing cases again (no full-time study until August!) and you will practice outlining and debriefing. None of this will be easy, so you need to manage your stress, anxiety and burnout. I have provided a checklist below so you don't forget anything.

March through July Checklist:

1. Read Chapter Three of "I Failed the UFE! Now What? A survival guide."
2. Come to terms with being an experienced writer. Say it out loud! (If you need help, find a sports psychologist to work with.)
3. Plan a vacation, long weekend trips, and evening adventures.
4. Practice sleeping! If you're not a good sleeper come up with a solution.
5. Practice the outlining approach. A strong outline will ensure a strong response.
6. Practice the debriefing approach. A detailed debrief will ensure you improve everyday.

Have other action items for March through July? Use the following pages to write them down:

March to July action items (Cont.):

March to July action items (Cont.):

CHAPTER THREE QUIZ: READY, SET, GO!
Are you ready?

Read the following questions and answer as honestly as possible on a scale of 1 to 5. (1 = Never 5 = Always)

1. I can say "I'm an experienced writer" out loud without fainting from embarrassment.

    1   2   3   4   5

2. I have been through this before and I have a lot more experience than the first-time writers. I know I can do this.

    1   2   3   4   5

3. I don't have to study more to pass the exam, I have to study smarter and I'm well organized to make this happen.

    1   2   3   4   5

4. I have a sports psychologist, or alternative, and I'm looking forward to talking to him/her. I know that it's going to help motivate me to the UFE finish line.

    1   2   3   4   5

5. I have written out affirmations and whenever I feel anxiety coming on I take a deep breath and say them to myself. I am in control of my anxiety!

    1   2   3   4   5

6. I'm experimenting with what helps me sleep better, so that when the UFE comes around I'll be able to sleep through the night.

    1   2   3   4   5

7. I am taking long weekends off this summer and I can't wait!

    1   2   3   4   5

8. I have a vacation booked for the week after the UFE. Now that's what I call a light at the end of the tunnel!
       1   2   3   4   5

9. I'm determined not to get burnt out and I know that if I start to feel it coming on I have to back off for an afternoon—or two!
       1   2   3   4   5

10. I know that debriefing is the key to passing the UFE, so I'm going to concentrate on my debriefing skills. This will increase my confidence too, because I'll be learning so much.
        1   2   3   4   5

NOW ADD UP YOUR POINTS AND SEE WHERE YOU FIT IN BELOW!

If your score is between 10 and 24: *You are working hard on your confidence, and it's working!*

You're feeling confident. Having confidence in your ability to pass the UFE is one of the most important aspects of success. Of course you have to study and know what you are doing, but all the studying you do this summer will mean nothing if you don't have confidence. So good for you! You are making sure that you stay confident throughout the summer.

If your score is between 25 and 39: *You know that you have to work at your confidence, and you are trying. But you don't feel totally confident—yet!*

Feeling confident takes work, and you are working on it. Having people to talk to, vacations planned, and keeping your anxiety low will help keep your confidence high by keeping everything in perspective. You are doing great at incorporating things into your schedule that will help you deal with stress and anxiety, and ultimately your confidence.

Your exercise: Continue to remind yourself that confidence is of the utmost importance for passing the UFE. Make sure you can identify the difference between real confidence and fake confidence (fake confidence: pretending that you feel great when you actually feel high anxiety) and if you start to feel low confidence, try discussing it more openly with someone. By being honest about how you feel you will be able to identify the reason you feel that way, and transform your feelings into a confident new you!

If your score is between 40 and 50: *You lack the confidence you want and need.*

Feeling confident really does take work, so don't feel discouraged if you aren't feeling confident in your UFE abilities. Failing the UFE has been hard on your ego, and that's normal. But now is the time to shake that feeling and empower yourself.

Don't let the UFE beat you, this is your year to win the UFE game. Take action!

All the little things that you learn in Chapter Three, like outlining skills, debriefing skills and having someone to talk to will help to improve your confidence. In addition to boosting your confidence, having someone to talk to, such as a good friend or a psychologist, will help you to identify the reason you are feeling low confidence. As soon as you can identify why, you can start changing it.

Don't feel discouraged that you don't feel confident yet, because that won't help! Instead, make small steps towards a more confident you by doing this exercise:

Your exercise: You have the confidence within you; you just have to remind yourself to feel that way! Do the following three exercises, and you will find your confidence improves.

1. Read Chapter Three again: Make sure you understand outlining and debriefing because these are key to having a strong understanding of writing cases, which will help to increase your confidence.

2. Find yourself someone to talk to: Find someone you feel comfortable talking to. Not someone who you casually discuss things with, but someone who will really listen. You need someone who you can open up to. This might be your friend, wife, husband, partner, boyfriend or sister, or it might be a psychologist. Whatever works.

3. Write down three affirmations of why you have the ability to pass the UFE this year: Your affirmations might include that you have already been through this and know what to expect or that you are going to study smart this year. Whatever the affirmation, you know you are able to pass, it's in there! But you have to really believe it yourself so that your brain believes it too. Write down your affirmations and have them on your wall, in your bag or on your fridge, wherever you will see them regularly. Every time you see them, say the affirmations to yourself slowly and visualize each affirmation so that your mind can trust that they are true. Believe in yourself, because if you have made it this far, the UFE is a surmountable obstacle. You just have to believe it to make it happen.

Have your own ideas about how you are feeling? Use the next few pages to write them down, along with what you can do to take action!

March to July - ideas, feelings, actions:

March to July - ideas, feelings, actions (Cont.):

March to July - ideas, feelings, actions (Cont.):

"One important key to success is self-confidence.
An important key to self-confidence is preparation."
- Arthur Ashe -
Professional tennis player

CHAPTER FOUR: AUGUST
What to expect

Getting to Competent
Come on already!

I'd be lying if I said that I wasn't nervous in August when I wasn't hitting Competent all the time. In fact I was very nervous. I kept thinking "Come on already! Let's do this!" I would analyze why I was still finding it hard to reach Competent in my second year and wonder what it meant about my ability to pass the UFE. Did it mean I was going to fail again? I had been told by several people several times that I wouldn't (and shouldn't) hit Competent consistently until it was time to write the UFE, but that didn't keep me from wanting to be there NOW!

To stay confident, I compared my case results to how I had done during the same week in the previous year. The differences were noticeable, not huge, but without doubt I was doing better than I had done the year before. This allowed me to stay confident in my ability to continue to progress, however slowly. So, if you find yourself getting impatient about getting to Competent, then compare how you are doing now to how you were doing at the same time last year. And remember what everyone always tells you: you won't, and should not, be getting to Competent consistently until it's time to write the UFE.

Remember: Getting good at the UFE is a slow process. Take it one step at a time. If you stay confident, follow the plan, and debrief well every time, you will pass the UFE!

Like I said in Chapter Three, this is just like running a marathon. It takes a lot of training and unfortunately it's the same in the second year. It doesn't just happen. You may start getting Competent regularly at the beginning of September, but not in August, and that's a good thing! You want to be able to peak on the actual UFE. It will happen, you just have to be patient.

I remember when it suddenly started getting easier for me, it was so exciting. I was hitting Competent! This might happen for you too, but don't get discouraged if you never consciously notice it. I spoke to several successful experienced writers who said that they never consciously noticed a shift, but they still passed. Make sure you are not stressed out and that you are following your study schedule, and you will start to hit Competent soon enough.

Competency Based Marking

UFE study can be very frustrating, especially to experienced writers. Because of the way competency based marking works you have to have all of the required elements to score a Competent rating. Therefore, you can be 90% of the way towards getting to a Competent and still have the same result as a candidate only 10% of the way towards scoring a Competent rating. This is why candidates talk about suddenly scoring better, which is how I felt. It's because they were getting better all the time but it only shows when you are 100% of the way there.

Have a Routine
Routines keep you sane!

Having a routine as an accountant is something that's hard to do because of work commitments and overtime. However, you have the time to get into a routine this summer and your body (and your UFE results) will thank you for it. When September comes around you will be in tip top shape for the UFE.

What I mean by having a routine is that you should be studying during the same time period every day, eating well, getting a lot of sleep, and exercising. If you like exercising and you do it regularly, make sure you do it during the summer on a regular basis too. You shouldn't be too busy to exercise because you are only studying during the day for seven to eight hours, so don't make excuses. Your body will appreciate being able to move. It is so easy to say that you don't have time to work out and brush it off, but the fact is that you are in a much better mental state when you exercise and being mentally healthy is essential to success on the UFE. Even if going for a twenty minute walk is all you can do every day, make sure you do that.

If you are used to going to the gym for an hour every evening, then continue to do that while you are studying for the UFE. Being on a schedule of eating, sleeping and exercise will make your body primed and ready to perform at its highest potential!

Stay on Track
Don't deviate from your study schedule

Are you sticking to your study schedule? If not, why not? If you aren't staying on track, take action now. It's not too late! If you notice yourself skipping cases, start writing it down every time you do. By putting your avoidance on paper you can't hide from it. If you notice you are skipping a lot, make sure you figure out why so you can stop skipping cases and start really studying for the UFE. You need to study to be ready to pass!

Helpful Hint: At the end of the week, review the list of any studying you have missed and determine why you skipped, then make an action plan to keep yourself from skipping for the same reason next time. If it's because there is nobody to meet at the library, then you need a study partner. If it is because you are feeling demotivated, you need to talk to someone. Remind yourself that although it's hard work now, it will be worth it when you pass! Don't give up.

Lacking Motivation

While I was studying in my second summer I had to fight the urge to give up. Sometimes I just wanted to get up and walk out of the library. I remember thinking to myself "Why am I doing this? I don't really care about getting my CA, I'm going to quit." I would almost believe it, but fortunately I am too stubborn to quit and I'm certainly glad of that. August seemed like such a long month of studying and dealing with the emotional stress of rewriting the UFE, so it was easy to convince myself that it was impossible. But it's not impossible. I passed, and you will too!

There was a man from my firm who was rewriting with me. I didn't know him very well but I had a friend who did. At one point she told me that she was concerned about him because he seemed to have just given up. He stopped returning her phone calls and was generally uninterested in pursuing the UFE any further. He sometimes studied, but had essentially given-in to failing again. When I heard this I totally understood what had driven him to that point: the pressures of studying all summer intermingled with the stress of having previously failed is hard to overcome and it would be easy to give up. On several occasions I felt like I didn't want to deal with it anymore, that I didn't want to write the UFE again, and that I just wanted to throw in the towel. But I always pushed through it, and for that I am thankful. Make sure you do too!

Got Motivation?
What to do if you start to lose your motivation

If you start feeling demotivated in August consider whether you are burnt out, you aren't sleeping well, you are experiencing high anxiety, or any other issue. Make sure that you deal with the issue appropriately so that you can push yourself through the wall and continue successfully.

Consider why you are feeling the way you feel and motivate yourself past it. Visualize how it would feel to give up and how much you will regret it a year from now if you do. If motivating yourself over these hurdles isn't working, don't be afraid or too proud to ask for help. Friends, family, your study partners or a psychologist can help you through this slump. Everyone needs a little help sometimes, so don't be afraid to ask for help.

To motivate myself I said my affirmations, thought positively, and always talked myself up. Talking positively to myself about my situation was really helpful. Never let yourself talk negatively to yourself or to others about the UFE.

August and September are tough with a lot of studying and a lot of mental barriers to push through. But you can do this. When I thought I couldn't I did, and I am here to tell you that you can too. This is your year to pass the UFE. *If I can do it, you can too!*

℞ *Remember: Don't be too proud to ask for help. Staying motivated is your main concern. I certainly could not have passed the UFE on my own.*

Too Much Study is bad
It causes burnout!

An extended study plan is often the cause of burnout. Studying too much and starting too early can be detrimental to your ability to pass. Every year I have students who tell me that they are going to start studying at the beginning of July because that's what's right for them, and inevitably they burn out. Two and a half months is just too long. The secret to passing the UFE is balance, so the March to June period is about laying the foundations back down so that you can get the most out of your UFE course in July. Passing the UFE requires no more than four to five weeks of intensive study for most students, which should have you peaking at just the right time before writing the actual UFE. See the Appendix (on Page 219) for the suggested study schedule.

℞ *Remember: More study is not the answer. Better, smarter study is what is crucial to UFE success.*

Being Positive
Always talk positively about the UFE

If you send your brain positive messages then it naturally looks for positive messages. If you keep sending it negative messages, then it will look for negative messages. You have to be conscious of finding something positive in each simulation debrief and always take away at least one positive thing at the end of each study day. Positive thoughts get positive results.

Now Let's Review...

On the following pages I provide a review of all the important things I covered in Chapter Three. This is a reminder that these things (markers, anxiety, burnout, to name a few) are extremely important, especially in August. And there's lots of new information too!

Having a Marker

As I discussed in Chapter Two, having at least one person to mark your cases is important for two reasons: You can compare how you mark yourself to how the marker marks you and it gives you an opportunity to receive notes to speed along your improvement. A marker can either be a person from your firm, an independent marker you hire, or your study partner.

Comparing your marker's mark to your own is important because you could be marking yourself too hard or to easily, and both can negatively affect your progress. If you are marking yourself too hard (i.e. you only just got to Reaching Competent, so to be on the safe side you give yourself a Nominally Competent) you will decrease your confidence because you will feel as though you aren't doing very well. If you mark yourself too easily (i.e. you almost got Competent, and the one thing you missed you did have on your outline, so you give yourself a Competent instead of a Reaching Competent) then you will not be doing enough debriefing. If it happens once or twice and the difference is minimal it's okay. But if it happens all the time, then be careful. Ask yourself why so that you can improve your marking accuracy on your subsequent cases and get the most out of your confidence and your debriefing.

Have people mark your exams once or twice a week in August and September, up to the second to last week of studying. Consider having a few different markers so that you can get your exam back in a reasonable time, and so you can get feedback from more than one person.

Remember: *Although it is embarrassing to send in a case that you didn't do well on, it is also the best case to have marked because it gives you the most opportunity to learn from the marker's comments. There isn't much a marker can tell you if you get Competent across the board. So instead of feeling embarrassed remember that it is a learning experience!*

If you're not getting your cases back in a reasonable time, then stop sending cases to that marker. A marked exam one week later is much less helpful than two days later. Have an agreed time limit with your marker so that you are both clear on the expectations of when it should be returned.

Take the markers comments to heart. Sometimes they will notice something that you haven't noticed, so take note. Consider why you did it, if you always do it, and how you can integrate the markers suggestions into your next response. If it's something significant, write it down on a post-it note and stick it above your desk so that you can embed it in your memory. Once it is ingrained and you always remember, you can get rid of the post-it note and impress your marker the next time they mark a response and the weakness is gone.

Marking
If you're not at a Big Four firm, consider hiring a marker

Marker support for candidates within Big Four firms is often an integral part of their study support system. However, for candidates outside of Big Four firms (and that's the majority of experienced writers) it is not always practical, or possible, to have any marker support within the firm. For these candidates you have the option of your study partner marking some cases, any firm practice exams that are marked externally, and hiring a marker. In addition, if you take a course in July, compare your marking at that time as well. If you do not have a marker, seriously consider hiring someone to independently mark for you in August and September. Having a marker is an extremely important aspect of ensuring that you are marking yourself accurately. Some markers provide mentoring services as well.

Remember: *Marking yourself too hard is bad because it decreases your confidence, and marking yourself too easy is bad because then you don't do a detailed enough debrief. Having a marker helps you to ensure you are marking yourself just right, by comparing the mark you gave yourself to what the marker gives you.*

Burnout and Anxiety
Identify and Monitor Your Burnout

The repetitive nature of studying for the UFE and the stress of the looming three days is a lot to deal with, so don't underestimate the importance of keeping your burnout and anxiety in check. Do whatever it takes to stay anxiety free and to avoid burnout.

While I was studying there was a time when I couldn't retain any technical and I felt bored and tired. I wanted to review technical all afternoon, but I wasn't retaining anything. I realized that I was burnt out: I was tired, stressed and overworked. I had been told by a few people casually to make sure I didn't burnout, but I didn't know how to tell if I was. However, from my lack of retention I decided that it was best to take the afternoon off and come back fresh the next morning. And so that's what I did. I packed up my bags, phoned a friend and went to the beach for the afternoon. The next day I felt so much better. I was refreshed and able to retain information.

I also started to experience burnout the week before the UFE on my second attempt. The more I studied the more burnt out I felt. I wasn't going to let this whole summer of studying go to waste by getting burnt out, so, for the last couple days I only studied in the mornings and that was enough to keep my mind fresh without burning out. This was easy for me to do because my study schedule was left open for my last week of studying, as it is on the sample study schedule in the Appendix (on Page 219), allowing me to study the way I needed to in the last week without missing out on important cases.

I cannot emphasize enough how important it is to monitor your burnout. If you are getting burnt out and just don't feel like studying anymore then don't study! This sounds a bit ridiculous, I know, in a summer when your full time job is studying. But it is so important to the success of the UFE.

Burnout and anxiety are the culprit for so many people who fail the UFE, so learn from their mistakes and take a break when you need one. Of course you shouldn't just leave early every day because you aren't motivating yourself enough, that's a different situation so make sure you can tell the difference between burnout and lack of motivation!

There weren't many times when I got burnt out because I was careful not to study on the weekends or in the evenings and I only studied for six and a half hours a day (seven hours including a half hour lunch break.) I always had something fun to do on the weekend and I kept busy during the week. And you should too. This will keep you relaxed and burnout-free. By keeping busy you are forcing yourself to think about anything but the UFE during the evenings and on the weekends.

Based on the traditional study schedule, the optimal study period is four weeks, so serious UFE study will start in mid August. By keeping the study period short and focused you prevent a lot of burnout issues, and you peak at the right time. To prevent burnout it is absolutely crucial that you have a balanced study day and that there is no night or weekend study. It is also crucial that you have a distinct non-UFE life with things to do in the evenings and weekends. All of these things reduce the chance of burnout becoming a factor.

Anxiety
No heart palpitations allowed!

On Page 111 in Chapter Three I provided examples of affirmations that I used in my repeat summer. If you are experiencing anxiety, make sure that you have affirmations that work for you and say them when you feel your anxiety rise. Wherever you are you can say them out loud or in your head, both are just as effective. Notice your heart rate starting to decrease its pace and your stomach start to calm down. Review your own affirmations on Page 111.

Sports Psychologist
Visualize yourself passing the UFE

If you are dealing with serious stress management issues then you should consider finding a sports psychologist to help you to visualize passing the UFE and to give you exercises to manage your stress. Major sports professionals have sports psychologists to help them visualize and accomplish their goals and win. If you are really struggling with stress aspects then you should check your employers benefits package to see if it covers stress related counseling. If not, then you can also check to see if your Institute has any stress management programs in place that might assist you.

CHAPTER FOUR SUMMARY

August and September are very intensive. If you remain focused, relaxed, and motivated with fun adventures in the evenings and on the weekends, you will be a strong candidate as the UFE approaches. If you find yourself getting off track, don't give up. Take action! I have provided a checklist below so you don't forget anything.

August Checklist:

1. Read Chapter Four of "I Failed the UFE! Now What? An experienced writer's survival guide."
2. Don't get burnt out. Take time off if you need it and have a routine for yourself that includes sleeping and exercise.
3. Stay motivated. If you find yourself hitting a wall find out why and fix it. This is your year to pass the UFE!

Have other action items for August? Use the following pages to write them down so you can refer back at anytime.

August action items (Cont.):

August action items (Cont.):

CHAPTER FOUR QUIZ: ONE MORE MONTH TO GO!

Read the following questions and answer as honestly as possible on a scale of 1 to 5. (1 = Never 5 = Always)

1. I want to consistently get to Competent now, but I know it's not going to happen until the UFE and I'm okay with that.

   1   2   3   4   5

2. I love my marker! I always get my exams back within a few days, and the comments are relevant and helpful.

   1   2   3   4   5

3. I feel comfortable calling my mentor at anytime for support.

   1   2   3   4   5

4. If I start feeling burnt out I know it's time to take a day off.

   1   2   3   4   5

5. My anxiety is at a motivating level. Whenever I feel high anxiety I say my affirmations and my anxiety goes down.

   1   2   3   4   5

6. I have a good routine, and I feel confident that my routine is keeping me in the study mode and anxiety free.

   1   2   3   4   5

7. I'm visualizing success!

   1   2   3   4   5

8. I'm feeling motivated and ready to rock the UFE!

   1   2   3   4   5

NOW ADD UP YOUR POINTS AND SEE WHERE YOU FIT IN BELOW

If your score is between 8 and 15: *You know exactly what to do to rock this thing, and you are not taking any chances!*

Good for you, you have everything in place. You have support in your marker and your mentor, and you are staying anxiety free! It's easy to get burnt out, but you're not about to let it ruin your chances of passing the UFE this year. Stay positive, confident, anxiety free and keep everything in perspective and you will be ready for the UFE.

If your score is between 16 and 28: *You know what it takes, but you haven't totally settled in.*

But don't worry, because you're on the right track. With a few weeks to go you are trying to keep on top of your confidence and your anxiety, and you are satisfied with your mentor and study partner (or if you're not you're willing to replace them!) Make sure you are keeping your anxiety low and your confidence high because you can do this!

If your score is between 29 and 40: *A few weeks to go, and you still have nerves about passing. But don't freak out!*

Take a deep breath and stay calm. You still have time, but take action now because September is right around the corner. Make sure you are getting what you need from your marker, mentor and study partner and if you aren't say "Hasta la vista!" You don't need anything bringing you down this year, and if you aren't finding the support you need take action and find it elsewhere.

Your exercise:
- Take a moment by yourself in a quiet place.
- On a piece of paper draw a line down the center.
- On the left hand side write down everything that could be keeping you from being in a better place with only a few weeks to go. Maybe it's your mentor or your marker not giving you what you need. Maybe you don't like the location of where you are

studying, or you find yourself unable to study with your study partner. Maybe you have such high anxiety, you aren't able to concentrate on your studying.

- On the right hand side next to each issue you have just identified, write down an action plan. Is your anxiety high? Action: get back into your exercise routine. Is your mentor MIA? Action: find a new one (write down some possible names right now!)

Remember, you have the power. Take action now!

Have your own ideas about how you are feeling? Use the next few pages to write them down, along with what you can do to take action!

August - ideas, feelings, actions:

August - ideas, feelings, actions (Cont.):

"Unless you are willing to have a go, fail miserably, and have another go, success won't happen."
- Phillip Adams -
Australian broadcaster, film producer, and writer

CHAPTER FIVE: SEPTEMBER
It's finally here!

September
Are you ready?

Just before the UFE I began to hit Competent more regularly. What a relief! It felt so good to know that I was finally 'getting it.' I continued to follow my study plan, review my technical, and strengthen my weaknesses and each case became a confidence booster. Finally I felt like I was ready to write this thing. At last I felt ready to pass the UFE!

Everyone hits this point at a different moment. Some people don't even consciously realize that it is happening, but if you have worked on your technical, case writing, and emotional aspects of the exam this day will come at some point late in the study process. You can pass the UFE! And when you notice that you are beginning to become a stronger case writer and that you are starting to be confident in your answers, soak it up and enjoy it. You are now ready to write the UFE and win.

If you are worried that you aren't "getting it" evaluate. The first step is go to your tracker. What does your tracker say. This is important, because it takes the emotions out of it. Your tracker shows you the reality of your situation. If, after reviewing your tracker, you are not comfortable with where you are at, take action! Call your mentor. Discuss your situation with someone who can help you. What areas do you need to work on? Once you know, write out an action plan so that you can fix the situation. It's not too late! Take action NOW!

The Last Week of Studying

At the end of the last week before the UFE I realized that I was burning out. If you have attempted anything longer than a four week study plan then it's likely that you will feel this way too. If you notice this in your last week of studying that's okay. It means that you are peaking at the perfect time, right before the UFE. Don't force yourself to study more if you feel prepared, because if you're ready you're ready. However, don't stop studying either. You want to make sure you study every day at least a little, which will keep you in a routine and make sure everything you have learned stays fresh in your mind.

Helpful Hint: Studying less is okay, as this will ensure you don't suffer from burnout, but not studying at all will be detrimental. In the last week I always wrote at least one simulation, debriefed it, reviewed my technical, but then took the afternoon off if I needed a break.

The basic four week study plan has two study weeks in August and two study weeks in September. You need to have structure each week of study including the last week as it is the time when all of your hard work can be lost if you do not pull everything together properly. Too often I have students deviating from their study plan in this last week because the nerves start getting to them; they either want to study more to make sure they have studied everything, or they want to scale back to almost no studying so that they are rested. But don't do either. Stick to your study schedule for optimal results!

In the traditional study plan (see the Appendix on Page 219 for a sample) candidates write a Comprehensive simulation on Monday or Tuesday mornings. It is important to have a Comprehensive in the last week because if you have not attempted a Comprehensive for two weeks before the UFE, then it is quite possible that you can lose your "Comp writing edge". It should not be the prior year's Comprehensive because if you do badly it has the potential to destroy your confidence, so use one that you have written before (either this year or last year.) This week is about ensuring you know the process and building confidence.

If you write the Comprehensive on Monday, then on Tuesday you should debrief it and write one Non-Comp and debrief it, and Wednesday you should write and debrief two simulations and after this there should not be any new simulations attempted. On Thursday and Friday you should only write one simulation each day and these should be simulations that you have written before and that you know you will do well on so that you keep your confidence high.

Remember: *Don't pick simulations you did badly on in the past because if you do badly on them again it can destroy your confidence.*

There should not be any technical study on Thursday or Friday afternoon in the last week because what can happen is you see new technical that you don't know, and you freak out that you don't know your technical, and then you want to study all weekend! So don't study any new technical, only review the technical you know you know, i.e. the study notes you have been reviewing all summer. Anything new can destroy your confidence this close to the UFE.

Writing 2011 Cases
This is the UFE I failed and it's making me nervous!

Writing the cases from the UFE you failed is really scary. All sorts of emotions are likely to go running through your head. It's terrifying that you have to write a case from the UFE that you weren't able to achieve competent on. Students often get quite worked up over the first case from the UFE they failed because it is likely to bring back all your emotions of failing. You are not alone in this. But just dive right in, write the case, and prove to yourself and everyone that you are going to pass this year, and last year's cases aren't going to decrease your confidence. You'll notice that once you write them it's not so bad. It's the same as all the other ones after all! You can do it.

Freaking Out With One Week To Go

It is very common to start freaking out with just one week to go. But if you're freaking out with one week to go until the UFE then take control. You need to calm yourself and get prepared. If you have followed your study schedule and debriefed cases, worked on your technical and focused on your weaknesses, then you are going to be ready to write the UFE. Feeling nervous that it is approaching is totally normal! Why wouldn't you feel nervous that the UFE is coming up after waiting a year to write it again? Of course you are nervous. You are not alone in this. Every year I receive phone calls from nervous students who start doubting themselves with one week to go. You are not alone, but you need to take control of those emotions and turn them around.

Take action. Review your tracker to see how much you have improved from your first case in the spring until now. Repeat your affirmations and positive thoughts to yourself. Review your list of weaknesses and remind yourself how much you have worked on them and how they are no longer weaknesses. You can pass the UFE, remember that. Believe in yourself. Stay positive. Don't let yourself get freaked out with just one week to go.

The Weekend Before the UFE

Every year I have several students who call me the last week of studying and say that they are just going to do "a little" studying on the weekend. Every year, without fail. Why, after studying perfectly all summer would you study on the weekend before the UFE? Because you want to tie up loose ends, and make sure that you feel like you've done everything you possibly can do to pass.

Okay, I understand that. But don't do it. Not just a little. Not a lot. Not at ALL. No studying the weekend before the UFE, ever. And this is why. If you study on the Saturday and Sunday, by the time you write Day Three of the UFE you will have been studying and writing exams for eleven days straight. On Day Three you will be extremely tired after writing three days of cases. If you studied on the weekend and you are going on day eleven of studying and writing tests then you are going to be beyond extremely tired and will find passing the UFE very difficult. Day Three is when a lot of people falter because they are tired and don't have the energy to make it through the last day. Don't let this be you! If you are thinking of studying on the weekend, stop yourself. It's never a good idea.

 *Remember: Don't study the weekend before the UFE. No exceptions.*

To keep yourself from feeling like you need to study on the weekend, plan out your week carefully. Make sure you have reviewed everything you want to review and are able to leave the library with a clear head knowing that you've done everything you need to do.

Monday Before the UFE

This can be a stressful day. It's important that you go to the library for a half-day in order to stay in the routine of studying and to be prepared for Tuesday. Not studying on Monday and having a long weekend off can confuse your body and mind, making it difficult to perform to your full potential on Day One of the UFE. However, studying for the full day is not a good idea either. You need to have the afternoon off so that you are refreshed for Day One.

I was so nervous the Monday before the UFE that I had to fight the negative thoughts in my head and force myself to think positively. I knew that if I started thinking negatively now, all my hard work over the summer would be for nothing.

I remember a friend telling me the year before I wrote the UFE that the night before Day One she lay down on her bed and said to herself "I can't do this, I'm in over my head." And then she realized what she was doing. She was talking negatively about her abilities to pass and she knew this would be catastrophic to her results. She had to stop herself. She made herself sit up, take a deep breath, and really force herself to think positively. "You have come this far and you are so close," she said to herself.

And this is exactly what I did while I sat in the library knowing that the next day I had to write the UFE, and only positive thoughts could get me through. "You have come this far and you are so close" I said to myself. Deep down I knew that I could do it, and saying this helped to remind myself of that. I had every reason to feel confident.

There are several things that you can do on Monday morning at the library in order to be fully prepared for Tuesday. Day One of the UFE is the Comprehensive simulation, so some people suggest that you do an exercise with a Comprehensive paper on the Monday before Day One.

Comprehensive Exercise
And other confidence boosters

Choose one of the UFE Comprehensive exams from the last three years and outline it. This is a confidence exercise. By outlining it you will remind yourself that you can identify issues and rock the exam, without needing to write the entire Comprehensive (which you absolutely should not do!) Compare your outline to the evaluation guide and get excited at how prepared you are.

For me, this exercise wasn't appealing. I didn't want to get into a big Comprehensive exam the day before the UFE, even if it was just outlining. It just didn't feel right for me. Confidence was my biggest weakness the first time I wrote the UFE so I was very careful the second time to make sure that I didn't make the same mistake again. I worked on my confidence all summer, and the day before was crucial as well. However, the Comprehensive exercise is a confidence builder too, and it is used by UFE writers consistently with positive results so it might be right for you.

Because I didn't do the Comprehensive exercise, I had plenty of time to build my confidence in other ways, so I started by reviewing my tracker. I compared it to the prior year and took a nice big exhale. It was true, I was doing better compared to the year before. I couldn't help but smile, and say to myself "you are ready to pass the UFE!"

After I did this I wrote down the following:
1. I have studied hard all summer. I know how to write cases. I know how to hit across the board. I can pass the UFE.
2. I was so close last year, and I am doing better this year. I can pass the UFE.
3. I have studied my technical and my technical is strong. I know I can pass the UFE.
4. I have done this before, I know what to expect. I have advantage over the first year writers because this isn't new for me. I have experience! I can pass the UFE.
5. If something comes up and I don't know what to do, take a deep breath, because if I don't know it, nobody else does either. And imagine how the

first years feel! It's worse for them, because I have experience. I've done this before! I can pass the UFE.

5. I can do this. I am ready. I am prepared. I *will* pass the UFE.

These notes let me see for myself that I was ready, and that I had every reason to believe in myself, that I was going to pass the UFE this year. There was no reason, after all the hard work I'd put in, that I wouldn't.

I had been reviewing my technical notes all summer, and there was nothing in there that I didn't know. So, for another confidence booster I looked over my notes and reminded myself that I knew all the technical and the triggers that could lead to that technical.

Whatever you do on that morning, anything that builds confidence is great because you really do have to believe that you can pass. By reviewing my indicator tracker and writing down confidence boosters I was telling my brain to stop being nervous because I was ready. Then it was time to rest.

Monday Night Before the UFE

In August Todd and I built a row boat with some friends at the Vancouver Wooden Boat Festival on Granville Island. Admittedly, due to my study schedule and my unavailability during the daylight hours, I was only available for some of the boat building. However, it was a fun accomplishment and Todd finished painting it in time to launch it the Monday night before the UFE. While I was trying hard not to be stressed, Todd was in his post-accomplishment glory. He was so excited to launch his homemade boat.

The whole point of the evening for me was to keep my mind off of the looming UFE. As excited as I was about the boat, my primary mission was to not think about the UFE and with that I succeeded! Imagine a beautiful wooden boat that had just been handmade. It was a warm summer evening in Vancouver at Kitsilano Beach, and we were out on the water enjoying the perfect evening.... and then the oar holder broke! Great boat, cheap oar holders. We had only just begun our journey, so we were several kilometers from the dock space where we planned to leave the boat.

While I tried (without much success) to not link this bad luck to the UFE, Todd tried to paddle towards the dock space as if we were in a canoe. This was quite humorous for me to watch because we were so far away from the dock and we were moving very slowly, so making it to shore didn't look good. There was nothing much I could do to help out, however I did suggest we get some assistance from a fellow boat owner. Todd was not ecstatic about the idea at first but once reality hit that canoeing a row boat several kilometers was not going to be easy, he agreed with me and we flagged over a speed boat.

The speedboat that picked us up was charged by a single man who welcomed us very warmly. He tied our beautiful row boat to the back of his speedboat and towed it (and us) to the dock. We tied up the boat and had a long beautiful walk home. By the time I got into bed I had had a brilliant evening with so much to think about that I fell into bed and slept all night.

Tuesday
Day One

I woke up Tuesday morning excited. I felt ready for the UFE and ready to pass it. This was my year! I got up early and had a long shower and said my affirmations several times. I packed a lot of food and water and drove to the writing center to be there over an hour early. I knew where I wanted to sit and I knew I had to get there early if I wanted to choose.

As I arrived at my writing location, the same old feelings of embarrassment and disappointment came to me; what was wrong with me? Why did I have to write it again? But I pushed that out of my head as I grabbed a seat. I would only allow positive thoughts. When I had completed my setup I went outside for a walk.

I found a bench to sit on and I began to read my novel. It was hard to get into at first, but once I did it was the perfect way to forget about where I was. Before I went back inside I phoned Todd to get one last pep talk. He helped me boost my positive thoughts and reminded me to put a smile on my face and that I could do this.

I wrote my second UFE in 2008. The Comprehensive in 2008 felt hard. Everything

I had promised myself not to do I did. In the middle of my cash flow I realized I was taking way too long, which is exactly what I had promised myself I wouldn't do. More catastrophically the case was undirected and I didn't know how to outline for an undirected case. But I had worked so hard all summer, and I wasn't about to concede. All the positive talking had worked, because instead of getting freaked out that the question was undirected, I took a deep breath and just followed my outlining (that I had practiced and perfected all summer) as best as I could. "Everyone is writing the exact same question" I kept reminding myself. "Everyone is in the exact same situation. If they can do it, I can do it! It's much scarier for the first-time writers because they don't have experience!" If I had been negative, I never would have gotten through that.

And then it was over. I felt sort of like a robot packing up my things and leaving Day One. I was finally writing the UFE again and this was my chance to do it, but I didn't feel like I was off to a good start. As I drove home it took every ounce of strength to not start talking negatively to myself. Instead, I thought positively about the exam. I thought of all the positive aspects of what I had done on the case, making myself stay upbeat. When I got home I went for a run and continued talking positively to myself. Over and over again I repeated to myself something to the effect of "Today was hard, but that means that tomorrow will be easier. It will be more directed and I will do really well. Everyone wrote the same exam that I did today, and nobody was prepared for it being undirected. I have more experience than all of them so I am lucky!" Getting some exercise and talking myself up was essential to staying positive.

Helpful Hint: Think of all the positive aspects of the exam on your way home each day to mentally prepare yourself for the next day.

Tuesday Night

I absolutely insisted that I have plans each night of the UFE, and Todd was a great sport. On Tuesday night we cooked up a big meal with our friends and ate it on their rooftop patio overlooking the ocean. This was the perfect night after a ridiculously hard

Day One. And because they knew so little about the UFE I didn't have to talk about it, which was wonderful! What better way to keep me distracted than being around people who don't know anything about accounting! I went home early of course, because I wanted to make sure I had a good sleep. I was pretty tired from the exam so I went straight to bed and slept through the night.

Remember: Don't talk about the exam. When each day is over, leave it behind. Don't study either, just enjoy a fun evening with no UFE thoughts.

Wednesday
Day Two

Similar to Day One I arrived an hour early to my writing location so that I could sit in the same spot. It was pouring rain and I didn't have the car, so it was hard to get away from the chatter. I didn't want to hear people talk about Day One, but everywhere I went I could hear people discussing it. This left me no choice but to put my headphones on and listen to music in a corner. Although it was antisocial, I didn't care. All I cared about was staying calm, positive, and focused.

Before the exam started I called Todd and he gave me a nice pep talk, and then I wrote Day Two. It was directed! What a relief! It felt so easy compared to the day before and I felt so confident. When I got home and Todd asked how it went, I think I surprised him when I said that it was good. He had never heard me say that after writing any day of the UFE! I felt hopeful.

Wednesday Night

The plan for Wednesday night was to go for dinner after Todd was finished working. We decided to go to this great wine and tapas bar that we love. It was a nice relaxing dinner and a great way to celebrate how far I had come.

At 3 a.m. I woke up with a severe stomach ache. I couldn't believe that this was happening to me before Day Three of the UFE. As I was lying in bed with mild food poisoning, I started to feel sorry for myself, thinking 'this is going to ruin me and my chances of passing.' But, like I had trained myself many times before during the summer, I talked myself out of being negative. I just didn't allow myself to quit. "Remember," I told myself, "I can function remarkably well with very little sleep. Getting negative now will be much more detrimental than a few hours of lost sleep. Don't worry, you'll be fine."

H Helpful Hint: If you start feeling discouraged during the three days of the UFE, repeat positive thought and affirmations. You've come this far, don't quit now.

Thursday
Day Three

I woke up on Thursday morning groggy and tired. I hadn't slept much the night before because of my stomach, and I still felt sick. I kept pushing back my fears because I wasn't going to give up when I had come this far. I popped a pain killer, washed my face with cold water, and drove to the writing center.

Once again I arrived an hour early. After setting up I sat in my car reading and listening to music. I was listening to my sister's album, Aspen Switzer (check out her music at www.AspenSwitzer.com. A shameless plug of my favourite singer!) The song that I was listening to is called "What Will Be". In the song there is a line that says; "and what will be will be, but now I know, there's an unshakeable seed, at the center of my soul."

That is exactly how I felt. I had been through a lot in the last year. I had failed the UFE and felt like my world had blown up right in front of me, but I was coming out the other end a better and stronger person. I would never again judge anybody for not doing well on something. After failing the UFE I came to understand that sometimes things happen that aren't expected and don't necessarily reflect on someone's ability. I made it through the year. Here I was. I had come this far. I was ready for Day Three and I was going to fight to the bitter end. But "what will be will be." Failing again would be horrible and I would be devastated, but I wasn't going to go down without a fight. And if I did go down, I had succeeded with one thing. I was a better person for having gone through everything that I had endured, and I was more understanding and accepting.

I walked from my car into Day Three with these positive thoughts in my head, and I was determined. I was going to win this game.

As a fun show-of-support Todd made me and my friend, who was also writing, a present. Over the years I have tried to explain to him what I do both at work and while studying for the UFE. It's not always easy to explain or understand, but he is interested and tries his best. On Wednesday afternoon he made us little paper hats. On each side of the hat he drew a bow and arrow and wrote underneath "The Indicator Hunter." I handed my friend her Indicator Hunter Hat that Todd had made, we had a good laugh, and then it was time. This was going to be my final day writing the UFE. I was determined of that!

I opened the exam and it was Day One all over again, but worse! Day Three was undirected, just like Day One, and after Day Two being so directed I wasn't prepared for it mentally, in addition to being tired and sick. I couldn't concentrate. I was so tired and I had to fight to keep myself from daydreaming. I felt like I was swimming through the ocean and couldn't find the surface.

And then it was over. Day Three was over. The UFE was over. As the papers started to get collected, my heart sank. I had blown it. There wasn't a doubt in my mind at that point. I looked over at my friend who was sitting beside me and she knew what I was thinking. She told me not to worry, that she felt the exact same way. It was everything I could do to not break down in tears right then and there. I got to my car as fast as I could and drove out of the parking lot and as soon as I was out of sight, I started to cry. If I had felt relatively confident the year before, now I felt like this year there was no way that I could have passed. "What's the matter with you?" I said to myself. "Now you're right back to where you started."

Todd was so excited that I was done and he thought that Thursday would be a big celebration. He had a card for me saying congratulations and he was at home and ready to pop the champagne. But I couldn't celebrate. I was so upset. I was convinced that I had failed.

We were going out for dinner and I decided I should walk by myself and meet him there to clear my head. I didn't want to talk to Todd about the UFE. I didn't want to celebrate. Nobody could possibly understand what I was going through. I felt so ashamed.

In hindsight I suppose it isn't that surprising that I was so upset, since I had been holding back all of my stress and fears for the entire summer. I had needed to talk myself up and be positive for months, and now the exam was over and I could let it all out. The stress of the whole summer, which I hadn't allowed myself to take on, was coming out in full force.

Todd's aunt and his sister met us for dinner and they were so sweet to me. They arrived with flowers and presents and treated me to a delicious dinner. They were so excited, and regardless that I thought that I had failed they didn't care. They said that we were celebrating that I had finished writing, and for now that's all that mattered. And so we celebrated, and it did feel good!

 *Remember: Celebrate on Thursday night. You deserve it!*

Holiday Time!

The next day Todd and I flew to Montreal for a few nights and then drove down to New York City. What a relief to have a holiday planned. It was the perfect way to get me over the misery of feeling like I had failed again. That was important for me. If I had gone back to work on Monday morning I would have underperformed due to all the stress and the jitters. There is so much build-up to the UFE, so to have to go back to work immediately without winding down would be difficult, even more so than writing my first year. I recommend at least going on a little mini holiday if that's all that you can do, and most firms are understanding and give you at least some time off after the UFE. You need a break!

SUMMARY

Be prepared with fun things to do the week you are writing the UFE. You want to make sure that when you aren't writing the exam you aren't thinking about it. And prepare yourself mentally for each day of writing by being strong and positive. I have provided a checklist below so you don't forget anything.

September Checklist

1. Read Chapter Five of "I Failed the UFE! Now What? A survival guide."
2. Don't burnout.
3. Have a plan for each afternoon and evening of the UFE.
4. Organize a holiday after the UFE so that you can go away. You deserve it!

Have your own ideas about how you are feeling? Use the following pages to write them down, along with what you can do to take action!

September action items (Cont.):

> "Success is not final, failure is not fatal: it is the courage to continue that counts."
> - Winston Churchill -
> British politician

CHAPTER SIX: RESULTS
Waiting (again) and the excitement of passing

The Wait is On

Waiting the second time was much harder for me. I felt like there was a lot more on the line because I had failed once before and on top of this, I wasn't feeling confident about passing. But as October became November my stress and anxiety had decreased to a more manageable level. I'm sure you remember what it's like: waiting is hard, but the less I thought about it the faster time went. Sometimes I would do a mental calculation in my head and think "only five weeks left and then I'll know!" But the less I thought about it, the better I felt.

I started doing a lot of yoga and would go to class most nights after work. I always left feeling great and the better I felt about myself, the less I worried about my results. Although you might not be interested in yoga (but don't knock it until you try it!) staying busy is just as important now as it was during the summer. It's not going to change your results on the UFE of course, but it will minimize any negativity and stress about your results. This will help your performance at work and keep you from feeling negative in your everyday life.

Making Changes and Staying Positive

Change is good. Change is hard. I had not been happy for two of the three years I had worked at my firm and Todd had been begging me to quit almost since I had started. I was surviving, but just barely. I needed a change.

I didn't feel like the same person when I returned to work after my second UFE summer. I had been through so much in the previous year, and I was ready for a new job. I liked what I did most of the time, but I didn't fit into the firm and I was ready to work in a firm where I did. Before rewriting the UFE I didn't want to quit because I felt like I would be letting the firm down, but after repeating the UFE I realized that staying with my firm was not good for me, and that's what I needed to focus on. So, in the time that I waited for results I was working a lot, looking for a new job, and generally trying to think about anything but the UFE.

I don't know if I would have made the change to my new job if I hadn't repeated the UFE, which made me realize that if I didn't pass there was still something positive coming from failing. I was definitely a stronger person and although it wasn't worth it to rewrite the UFE just for that, it sure was an unexpected bonus. I am not saying that whether you pass the UFE or not doesn't matter because it's a learning experience. The purpose of writing the UFE again is to pass (obviously!) What I am saying is that you studied all summer and you wrote the UFE and now it is out of your hands, and it makes waiting that much more bearable if you allow yourself to see the positive changes your experience has allowed for.

Getting a New Job
If you want one, get one

Students tell me all the time that they won't be able to get a job because they failed the UFE. Although it might be true that some firms won't hire you because you failed, you don't want to work for them anyway (they are just being short sighted). Many firms do hire students who have failed, and not only *after* they have passed on a repeat attempt. It is not uncommon for firms to hire students before they have passed the UFE. So if you want or need a new job, then go ahead and apply!

You Don't Know Whether You Passed or Failed
Don't let negative feelings take control. Be positive!

Although most days I felt certain I had failed again, I made every effort to be positive after writing the UFE. Months later I was talking to a friend over coffee and related my UFE experience to her, saying that I thought I had failed (which I describe in Chapter Five.) She said she was surprised I'd felt that way because she hadn't noticed, which is exactly what I was trying to accomplish. I wasn't trying to hide my feelings from my friends, I was simply not letting the emotions of Day Three convince me of something I couldn't possibly know. There was no way I could say with any certainty whether I had passed the UFE or not. The fact that I felt like I had failed was not a good enough indication of the actual facts. I insisted to myself that I continue to be positive.

Thinking positively is easier said than done. I have this strange idea that if I think positively then I am going to set myself up for failure, but as I have said throughout this book, thinking positively is essential. Thinking positively during the summer and throughout the three days of the UFE gives you the power to pass the UFE and thinking positively now is just as important. While it won't change your UFE results, it will make the time in October and November pass more quickly. Be positive, because there is no way for you to know the outcome of your results.

I always hear from students after the UFE who say that the UFE was the hardest it's ever been, that there's no way they could have passed, and then they start discussing immediately the action plan for writing again the next year. But this is all emotion talking. Everyone wrote the same UFE. It's always hard! People think they fail all the time who end up passing. So don't let the negative feelings spiral you into planning your study schedule for the next UFE before results come out. Think positively, and the time will go by faster. And really, you just never know whether you passed or failed. Going on feeling is never a good enough indication to know your results.

The Time Has Come
Results

When results came out I had just started a new job. I could have pretended that this was my first attempt, and not told anyone that I had failed the year before, but I didn't want to revert back to feeling ashamed about it, so I was not only the new girl, I was the new-girl-who-had-failed-the-UFE-the-year-before.

I was really nervous. What if I failed again? I had a hard time concentrating at work in the week leading up to results. I sat across from the only other UFE writer at the firm, so sometimes we would discuss results. I had a few moments of relief from my stress when he told me how upset his girlfriend was for not having achieved honour roll, and we had a good laugh. Honour roll! If only that was my concern.

And then it was Thursday night. Todd was out of town for work so my sister, Aspen, (yes, that Aspen. www.aspenswitzer.com) came to hang out with me. We went for a great sushi dinner and then to a movie. It allowed me to forget for moments at a time the enormity of the next morning.

And then it was morning. As I explain in detail on Page 195 in Chapter Seven I was so excited upon seeing my successful results that I grabbed Aspen and jumped up and down screaming "I passed!" I remember at MPAcc my accounting teacher once saying that the day he passed the UFE was the best day in his life. I remember thinking, 'come on, that's a bit much' but after having felt the joy of passing I have to say I understand. I had a permanent smile on my face for at least two weeks.

That is the moment that you work towards. The jumping up and down, the smile, and the relief. That smile that takes over your face upon passing the UFE is unparalleled. It just can't be beaten.

SUMMARY

Get involved with whatever you love so that you have less time to think about the UFE results. When you see your number on the screen saying 'Competency Achieved' feel free to jump up and down!

October and November Checklist

1. Read Chapter Six of "I Failed the UFE! Now What? A survival guide."
2. Be positive.
3. Stay busy.
4. Have something planned for the night before UFE Results.

Use the next few pages and to write down any thoughts you have, ways to stay busy, and overall how to keep your sanity.

September to December (Cont.):

"You are now the world's finest Olympic Coach. Your CA is your Olympian and your job is to help them win Gold."

- Todd Allen -
Supporter of successful experienced writer

CHAPTER SEVEN: FOR THE "SUPPORTERS-OF"
Ask the people in your life to please read this!

An Introduction by Todd Allen
From one supporter to another

My name is Todd Allen and I hate the UFE. I'd be willing to bet that you hate it too. Not to worry, these feelings are totally reasonable and justified. Two years after my wife Kayla (the author of this book) finally finished panicking, studying, panicking, studying, failing, panicking, studying, panicking, writing for the second time, crying and then ultimately passing as an experienced writer, I still loathe the UFE with every ounce of my being.

That one little test brought our relationship to the brink of disaster. What is it about that exam that turns normal human beings into fire breathing dragons? To this day I don't know the answer.

My intention here is to help you, the supporter. I want to lessen the pain that you are going through right now. Sure, I care about the UFE writers and that's what this book is all about. But let's be honest; you are probably enduring far more suffering (FYI: don't tell them you think that.)

There are two ways to approach another UFE summer with your UFE writer ("your CA"). Option One: You can throw up your hands and tell your CA to suck it up when they start acting crazy (but remember to duck after saying this.), or Option Two: You can attempt to give your CA everything he/she needs so they can pass this exam quickly and with confidence so you don't have to hear about the UFE ever again.

Obviously option two is the best choice if you care about your CA, and clearly you do if you're reading this section of the book. So if you want to follow option two, here it is. This is all you have to do. It's very simple and if acted upon immediately this piece of information will greatly improve your quality of life for the next few months.

What to do as the supporter
Go for Gold

You are no longer the mother, father, friend, girlfriend, boyfriend, wife, husband, partner or innocent and defenseless stranger of a UFE writer. You are now the world's finest Olympic Coach. Your CA is your Olympian and your job is to help them win Gold.

This isn't going to be easy. An Olympic Coach is always there for their Athlete. They are there for the early morning workouts. They are there for late night workouts. They are there when it starts to rain. They are there when the entire goal of winning does not even seem possible. An Olympic Coach never stops supporting their Athlete. An Olympic Coach never walks away early and never stops believing in their Athlete, not even for a second. Why do they do this when they are not the ones competing? Because the Coach wants to win Gold too.

Your CA's "Gold" is seeing the words "Competency Achieved" beside their name. And if they win Gold, you win Gold. Your Gold is never having to be woken up in the middle of the night because your CA can't sleep. Your Gold is never again having shoes, cereal boxes and hair brushes thrown at your head. Your Gold is never having to come home to see your CA sad and depressed, sitting on the couch with tears in their eyes and empty candy wrappers riddled throughout the floor. Your Gold is never having to hear or talk about this hideous, life disturbing, painstaking thing known as the UFE ever again. Can you imagine a world like that?

So snap to it, Coach. Give your CA everything they need to win Gold. It's only going to make it better for you.

Supporter of a successful experienced writer

Give Me Support!

Your CA has been going to school for years. So many years! If you are a significant other it's possible that your CA has been in school as long as you have known them. If you are a friend or family member, you know there was a time when your CA wasn't going to school but you don't remember it. The school, the exams, the articling. It can be exhausting. But for one more summer we need your support.

Todd is the reason that I have my CA. He took me out for dinner after I hit certain milestones, he took me on vacation after I finished the UFE (both times), and he was more nervous than I was the second time we waited for the results. Todd may not have been doing the studying and he wasn't required to pass the exams, but he was just as much a part of my CA education as I was. I needed his support and most literally could not have done it without him.

I also had my family. Although my family and I don't live in the same city, their support was invaluable to me. Weeks after failing the UFE my family continued to let me drone on about how sorry I was for myself. As my biggest supporters they knew that I would get over it and that I just needed some time.

I knew a woman who was writing the UFE for her third time, and even on her third attempt her fiancé wouldn't acknowledge that the UFE had anything to do with him. He shrugged it off, refusing to read the final chapter "Significant Others" in UFE Success by Bruce Densmore. Because it wasn't him that had decided to become a CA, he didn't feel responsible. His lack of support drove her to have low confidence and indifference, two of the most dangerous things when writing the UFE. She never did pass the UFE.

The Pressures of an Experienced Writer

In a profession where an excellent grade, a "perfect" personality, and an impeccable work ethic make you merely average (at best), failing the UFE is hardly something that can be forgotten. It's hard on the ego any way you slice it. Think of an exam that is being written by thousands of people across the country who have never failed a test before. Only

70%-75% of them can pass. That's the UFE. The UFE is the first exam that those who have never failed anything in their life might actually fail. This is what your CA is up against.

I remember reading an article in CA Magazine that focused on a man who had become a doctor after doing his CA. Even after medical school he said, "I still maintain that the UFE was the hardest exam I ever wrote."

Understanding the UFE is difficult without experiencing it firsthand. Understanding the pressure of being an experienced writer is impossible. Being empathetic is all we ask!

Put Away the Punching Bag
No arguing

Whether it's a family member or a significant other, everyone fights sometimes. Some people do it more than others, but it's human nature to have to fight things out. Unfortunately, when we are stressed the gloves come off more often. The more stressed you are, the more you argue, the more stressed you are, the more you argue… and the cycle continues.

Your CA has both an emotional and an educational burden this summer and stress does not mix well with this. You are the support system, so decreasing this stress is your challenge. Staying low stress and low anxiety is the key to passing the UFE, and because there are a lot of stresses this summer keeping it in balance is more important than ever.

Your job: Keep your CA in balance. Keeping your CA in balance means no unnecessary arguing, fighting or bickering. You need to just let it go. Bite your tongue! It might not seem fair, but your CA will appreciate it, and the long term benefit is that your CA will pass the UFE!

Close the Books
No weekend or evening studying!

Your CA should not be studying in the evenings or on the weekends. No exception. If you notice that your CA is studying evenings or weekends, talk to them about it. Ask whether they have a balanced study schedule and remind them about burnout.

You should expect your CA to study no more than seven to eight hours a day, five days a week. Sometimes UFE writers are pressured by their parents to study more, to cram it in on evenings and weekends. This increases their stress and causes conflict for the writers because they don't want to let their parents down, but they know they shouldn't study more. So if you are this kind of parent, be careful. Your CA understands that you want the best for them, but there are very specific guidelines around studying, and more studying isn't necessarily better. Trust your CA to know when enough studying is enough.

Remember: Under no circumstance should you be pressuring your CA to study in excess of the allotted time. If your CA studies too much, they will fail the UFE.

What Not to Say

I know it's hard to know what to say. Knowing what to say, however, is less important than knowing what not to say. Basic rule: don't say anything that could be construed by your CA as you not taking the results seriously. Basically, anything that could be construed as you not understanding what your CA is going through. I have given examples below of what not to say, because the best you can hope for is that what you do say is not what you shouldn't say. Here are some examples of things that people said to me that always made me cringe:

1. **"Get over it"**: After I had failed the UFE Todd was very supportive. But five days later he couldn't understand why I hadn't gotten over it. I got home from work and

was feeling sorry for myself one night, and he couldn't take it anymore. He told me enough was enough. "Get over it. You can write it again next year."

May I recommend: I understand that it's hard to deal with someone who is getting down on themselves continuously over a test. But this isn't "just a test", so your CAs feelings of self doubt and misery after failing might last for awhile. Tell your CA that you are prepared to support them in any way they need help.

Helpful Hint: It's a lot for you to take on by yourself. If your CA has a best friend, group of friends, or close family members, suggest that your CA talk to them too. Be delicate, because your CA might not want to share their stress with others, but it might be helpful. For me, I was able to talk to my sisters and my parents to give Todd a break from hearing about it every day. You could say something like, "I know you're embarrassed, but I know your sister would understand." This way you aren't saying you're not willing to help, but it at least gives your CA a suggestion of someone else to talk to.

2. **"It's not a big deal"**: Yes it is. It is a **huge** deal! I know what people mean when they say this, and I know that they mean well, but seriously. It is a big deal. By saying that to me, I felt like the person was undermining how awful I felt. When I failed it was a pretty big deal, and I'm sure it is for your CA too.

May I recommend: Be understanding. Say things like "I know this is a big deal for you, is there any way I can make it easier?" You might have to bite your tongue sometimes, I know Todd did. He was very much a gentleman and forgave me for moping around the house for weeks—or was it months? May I suggest you do the same? Let them have their moment to feel like their world is coming to an end. For them this is a real feeling, but it will pass.

3. **"In the scheme of your life, this is nothing"**: Yes, this may be true. But after failing the biggest exam of his/he life, your CA can't be expected to be totally rational, right? It's true, in the scheme of my life failing the UFE was not a big deal, and now that

it's over that extra year is nothing to me. But when I failed it felt awful. I was in so much pain. It meant everything to me. I was a year behind everyone I had gone to school with and worked with, and I felt completely alone.

May I recommend: Every adult knows that one year is a small piece of a bigger picture. But maybe a UFE writer who has recently failed is not in the mindset of their adult brain? It seems to me that when something significant happens in our life, whether it's positive or negative, we don't act in a reasonable way. In fact we tend to start acting more like a child and reason leaves us. May I suggest that a UFE writer who has just failed has a longer-than-normal year ahead of them, and it feels unimaginable that they will ever make it to the end? By saying that this is only a small part of a long life, you are not understanding their current mindset: that in the scheme of things this feels like everything. Instead, try to understand that this seems like a very long and significant year and support them through it.

4. **"This is a blessing in disguise":** Often the most challenging obstacles in life make us better people, but that doesn't typically matter at the time because it doesn't feel like a blessing without hindsight. I'll admit that for me rewriting the UFE was a blessing in disguise; I am a stronger and better person for it and I learned a lot. But when I failed the UFE, hearing this almost made my heart stop because at the time there was nothing about the situation that I considered a blessing.

May I recommend: Biting your tongue. You might be forgiven if you say it after your CA passes the UFE, but even this I'd be careful of. Although I have no regrets about failing the UFE now, I know that for many people it was a painful experience that they don't want to talk about even after passing. Ever.

5. **"Don't worry. You'll be fine":** I strongly recommend you don't say this. Ever. Your CA does not feel like this. Your CA will worry about the UFE, and the best way you can help is by being supportive and believing in your CA.

May I recommend: Keep it to yourself. You might get away with saying "You can do this!"

A Schedule for the Supporters-Of
A month-by-month timeline for what you should do

Hopefully you are reading this in December or January. If you are, then this chapter will help you stay sane all year. It's a long road ahead, so try to be patient. If you're reading this later on in the year, that's still good! You can be forgiven for your unruly behaviour up to this point and still come out on top. Just follow the simple schedule below. It's designed to give you guidance through the year so that you can know what to expect and how to be a supporter-of!

December and January

You are your CAs support mechanism. Whether your CA is your life partner, husband, wife, fiancé, son, daughter, brother, sister or friend, you are reading this because he/she has asked for your support. This is not an easy job because you don't understand what your CA is going through. Are you a CA who wrote the UFE and passed the first time? You don't understand what your CA is going through. Are you a CA who was hung-over on results day and misread your results and thought for two hours that you had failed? You don't understand what your CA is going through. Did you fail a college exam once? You don't understand what your CA is going through. The only way you can possibly understand failing is if you have failed the UFE before. And even then, we all have different experiences, so you may not understand your CAs experience even if you did fail.

Your job: Let your CA talk about feeling depressed over failing. It is completely acceptable (and expected) that your CA feels down about failing for the first few weeks at least, and maybe longer, and your job is to, (1) Empathize and (2) Let them talk. That's really all you have to do! And if you want, read this entire book, because it will give you more background on your CAs challenges, and a deeper understanding of what they will be doing this year.

February to July

Your CA has a lot to organize in order to be prepared for rewriting the UFE. Everything about rewriting is new to them and there is limited guidance as an experienced writer. In addition, it's busy season at work.

How can you help? Most likely there isn't much to help with because they have to do most of it on their own, but there might be little things like making dinner and taking them to the movies to help them de-stress and not think about the UFE.

Your job: Sometimes just knowing you are there for them is what your CA needs, so ask the question: "What do you need from me?" Todd asked me this in the spring before my second attempt and because he asked, I was able to tell him. Telling him what I needed made it easier on both of us.

Helpful Hint: Communicate to your CA what you need from them too. This way you can decrease stress with open communication.

August

Your CA will be studying every day for the last two weeks of August. As you know from last summer, studying for the UFE is a full time job. Your CA will be going to the library Monday to Friday for seven to eight hours a day. This is a hard job of course, since there is so much to learn. But the great thing about the UFE summer is that there are no evening or weekend hours to work, which means more time with your CA.

Remember: *No studying during the evening or on weekends. Studying too much can lead to burnout, which occurs a lot among experienced writers. To perform well your CA requires good writing skills and technical knowledge, and just as importantly your CA needs to be relaxed with low anxiety.*

Burnout
Is your CA burnt out?

Your CA may be experiencing burnout if you notice the following:

- **They seem uninspired:** Your CA doesn't care about passing the UFE anymore and doesn't care that the UFE is approaching.

- **Tired and irritable:** Your CA appears to be more tired and irritable than usual.

- **Always thinking UFE:** Your CA is unable to stop thinking about the UFE even on the weekends, seems unable to relax, and is stressed.

- **Too serious:** Your CA is unable to see the humour in that which used to be funny, or if you try to make them laugh, they cry instead.

- **Taking time off:** Your CA is skipping studying days regularly and/or has become indifferent.

J*our job: If your CA is burnt out don't just ignore it and hope it will pass. They need to know, and you might realize it before they do. If you suspect that your CA is burnt out, approach them. Tell them that you understand that burnout is a serious issue and could lead to failing the UFE, and that you want to help. If they don't* want your help, suggest that they talk to their UFE mentor or to their study partner. Whatever you do, don't let them brush you off. They will thank you for it when they pass the UFE.

September

The month of the UFE has finally arrived. Everyone's reaction to September is different. Your CA might get excited that it's finally time to write again, or he/she might experience increased stress. I remember being really excited to write the UFE again. I had been waiting to be able to write it for months and I wanted to just get it over with. The time had finally arrived and it was such a relief, but I was also nervous. I would think to myself; "What if I mess it up and fail again? What if I'm not ready?"

Studying in the first two weeks of September will be similar to the last two weeks of August and staying low stress is the key! Be the Olympic Coach.

The Day Before Day One

This will be a Monday. Your CA will do some light study in the morning and take the afternoon off. Make plans for the evening. Meet for dinner, go for a walk, or go play tennis. Whatever it is, make definite plans so that your CA can have something to look forward to without being too preoccupied by the looming UFE.

Help your CA ensure a good night's sleep. Many candidates dealing with stress and/or sleep issues arrange to have a massage each night before a UFE writing day. Either book your CA a massage, or give them one yourself (for extra bonus points.)

℞ *Remember: There should be absolutely no arguing. Arguing the night before can seriously weaken your CAs ability to sleep and do well the next day.*

Mornings

Day One, Day Two, Day Three

Be flexible if you can. Whether your CA wants breakfast with you or alone, let your CA do what works best so that they can fully concentrate on the big day ahead. Give your CA a ride or let them take the car, whichever is preferable to him/her. Make the mornings relaxed and care-free.

Evenings
Day One and Day Two

Plan something to do for each evening. Make the decision with your CA so that they have something to look forward to. Even better, if your CA likes surprises then make it a surprise. Go to a friend's house or have a nice romantic meal. Whatever is fun for them and doesn't involve talking about the UFE.

Evening
Day Three

It's over! Hooray! It's time to celebrate!! Maybe…

Your CA has been under extreme stress this summer. There has been a lot of studying and focus on staying anxiety-free. Now that it is all over the feeling might be overwhelming. When I finished writing the second time I was upset and in no mood to celebrate. Todd was confused because he thought we should be celebrating but I couldn't. I was confused too. "I should be excited," I thought. "I'm done!" But because the stress of the summer was finally gone, I was exhausted!

Of course, this is not always the case. Hopefully your CA will take it better than I did and be ready for a glass of champagne. If so, then make it special for them. It meant the world to me that I came home to a card and dinner plans. These little things make a big difference.

Holiday Time!

Now that the UFE is over, hopefully you and your CA can have a holiday. I cannot stress enough the importance of taking a week off for having fun. Go to Hawaii or Mexico to lie on the beach and relax. You both deserve it!

October and November
Waiting for Results

This was pure agony for me. Two and a half months of walking around with a smile on my face pretending that the UFE results were the last thing on my mind was hard. It's cruel and unusual punishment. The stress of waiting for results is probably just as acute for you as it is for your CA. I know that Todd was a lot more nervous than I was to get the results because he couldn't stand the thought of another UFE summer. But the time will pass. Try to keep busy on the weekends too so that the time goes by more quickly.

December
Results

Todd had to go out of town for work the week of results and would be arriving home at 10:30 a.m. the day of; three and a half hours after results were released in Vancouver. Knowing the feeling of failing in the previous year, I knew I didn't want to be alone just in case I failed again. Just as importantly I wanted to have someone to jump up and down with if I passed. This illustrates the perpetual support of my family. When I told my mom that Todd was going to be away she didn't even miss a beat; her and my dad would drive down to be the support (it's an eight hour drive and she has a very full-time job with a lot of responsibility!) And then we realized that my sister, Aspen, was coming to town, so she came a few days earlier than planned to be with me that morning. How lucky I felt to have a family that was so supportive.

Aspen and I went for a sushi dinner the night before results. Being preoccupied with that, and later a movie, worked exceptionally well at minimizing the fear I would occasionally feel. I was surprised to sleep through the night and wake up the next morning just before 7 a.m. Upon waking up I was terrified. I was literally shaking. I could hardly open my computer or type in the website to check my results. Before I looked for my candidate number I went to wake up Aspen. And then, with my shaking hands, I logged in to check my results.

"I passed!" I shrieked. "Aspen. I passed. I PASSED!!!" I grabbed her in a hug and we jumped up and down as I continued to shriek in her ear.

I had passed. It was over. I have never felt so relieved.

As I write this, it still makes me smile thinking of us somewhere between the kitchen and the living room jumping up and down. As I tried to call Todd (I was shaking so badly I could barely dial his number) I asked Aspen to double check the computer to make sure that I had looked up the right candidate number!

Todd was so relieved when I told him; it was his victory too.

And then I called my mom and dad. One year before, my mom had known within minutes that I hadn't passed because I didn't call, so this year I phoned as quickly as I could. My other sister, Bree, had already left for work but as soon as she heard I'd passed she called too. My entire family was there for me when I failed and equally so when I passed.

And so, that is what you have to look forward to. As a supporter-of you are going to be able to relish in the accomplishment of winning UFE Gold!

H Helpful Hint: If your CA has the book "UFE Success" by Bruce Densmore, read the last chapter. It's for you too! Bruce has a lot of experience with the UFE, so he can give you another perspective on being the supporter.

SUMMARY

You are reading this because you are the main (or at least one of the main) supporters for your CA. This is a crucial summer for you both, so work together. Be there for your CA in whatever capacity he/she needs, even if it just means biting your tongue. And ask what your CA wants! Before studying starts this summer make sure you talk to your CA about what he/she needs. Most importantly help make this summer fun.

Your Checklist:

1. Read Chapter Seven of "I Failed the UFE! Now What? A survival guide."
2. Read the whole book "I Failed the UFE! Now What? A survival guide." This will give you a deeper understanding of everything your CA is going through.
3. Ask you CA what they need from you this summer.
4. Try to understand what your CA is experiencing, and make sure you aren't putting undue pressure on them.
5. Plan fun adventures and date nights to keep your CA occupied and happy.
6. Plan a holiday (earn extra points by making it a surprise.)

"Keep in mind that neither success nor failure is ever final."
- Roger Ward Babson -
Entrepreneur and business theorist

CHAPTER EIGHT: EXPERIENCED WRITERS
Real stories from real experienced writers

Real Stories
You are not alone

This is the first book ever published exclusively for experienced writers. I knew that I wanted to write this book because I would have loved to have this resource when I was rewriting, and I knew that I wasn't the only person who felt so alone when I failed the UFE. I had no idea where to start when I first failed. I felt so alone and wondered if maybe I was reacting differently than others, and that maybe I was the only person who didn't know what to do to get started. But then I started talking to people and realized that that wasn't true. It wasn't unusual that I felt depressed, confused and alone because I had failed the UFE, and all the experienced writers I spoke to that summer said that they felt like that too, especially, I noticed, if I said it first. So the problem wasn't that I was different. The problem was that everyone was afraid to say how they really felt; afraid that they might look tenuous to others. We were all pretending we were fine, and instead of learning from each other and from other successful experienced writers, we were all learning everything for the first time, with no guidance.

I wanted people to know that they were not alone, so I wrote this book. I said to myself: "If I help one person, this book has done its job." Thus, the purpose of this book was to help one person. If that happened, it was worth it.

I get emails from students all year asking questions and requesting advice. It can be extremely lonely being an experienced writer, so I love that students feel comfortable emailing me for advice. (You can too, through my website www.KaylaSwitzer.com). I share some of these students stories below, so that you can learn from them and know that you are not alone.

This Student Had a Death in the Family and Lost Her Job
But she did not give up

Dear Kayla,

I have to say that receiving your book from a colleague of mine this week was a blessing in disguise. I want to sincerely thank you for your words of empathy, encouragement and courage at a time when I needed them MOST. I cannot express enough what a positive influence your book has had on me!

I have ordered a copy of your book to read and reread as I complete my journey as an experienced writer.

Thank you for taking the leap of faith to write this book and share with others who are and will in the future take a similar journey.

This candidate does not have an easy story to tell. In 2009 she was ready to write the UFE. But on the Monday night before Day One she received a phone call that her sister had passed away. Despite her extreme sorrow she was advised to write. This ultimately led to her first attempt resulting in a "Competency Not Yet Achieved".

One year later, one day before she began studying for the UFE on her second attempt, her accounting firm laid her off. She had lost her sister less than one year earlier, and now the emotional and financial stress of losing her job made her feel like it was impossible to pass the UFE.

But with further thought, she decided she wasn't ready to quit. She took the advice given in the book "I Failed the UFE! Now What?" and made it her duty to prove her firm wrong; that she could pass this test and that she was worthy of become a Chartered Accountant. She made an appointment with a sports psychologist to help boost her confidence and decrease her anxiety, she wrote out affirmations that she repeated constantly, and she worked hard all summer studying for the UFE.

She began to notice that the study days were actually something she looked forward to as it kept her mind off of her disappointment in losing her job and her grief in losing her sister. She began to see that she was strong, that her case results were promising, and she began to believe that she would pass. When it was time to write the UFE she emailed me to say this:

> I feel more confident this year. The work I have put in towards reducing anxiety and thinking positively is working! I have put together a cheer with my boyfriend (who is a first time writer this year), which makes me laugh every time! I am also using the affirmations. I know my technical! I stayed focused and studied hard! I have been here before - this is my advantage!!!

This is the perfect example of a candidate who is ready to pass the UFE. You can't pass the UFE without confidence, and this email emanates confidence!

A Male's Point of View

I have often wondered whether men can relate to this book, as it is based on emotions that men are less likely to admit to. However, this is an email correspondence I had with a man who wrote the UFE (and passed!)

> I just wrote the UFE for the second time. I wanted to let you know how helpful your book, "I Failed the UFE! Now What?" was. I empathized with the feelings you experienced right after failing, and I couldn't have even attempted to write this year without following your advice of constant positive thinking.
>
> The paragraph that I appreciate most though is when you discuss what it would be like if you failed for a second time. "Failing again would be horrible and I would be devastated, but I wasn't going to go down without a fight. And if I did go down.... I was a better person for having gone through everything that I had endured." I pride myself on not being results-based, and I know I could not have done anything differently leading up to the exam, so I really should be happy no matter whether I pass or fail. Of course in this case that's very difficult. But I will be proud of myself for going through this process again, pass or fail.
>
> My wife (much like Todd for you) along with an incredible family and group of

friends are there for me no matter what my result. Like your husband and family, they just wanted me to celebrate after I finished the exam, even though I think one of the days was (potentially) disastrous (like you did).

There were so many parallels between our stories. Being able to understand that a successful experienced writer had very similar feelings to mine throughout the process - from finding out I didn't pass last year to the last day of the UFE - allowed me to remain positive whenever I wrote a terrible practice case. It also allowed me to fight off negative thoughts that popped into my head during the exam. I think I read this helpful hint twenty times during the three day UFE period: "If you start feeling discouraged during the three days of the UFE, repeat positive thoughts and affirmations. You've come this far, don't quit now." After a very difficult Day Two where I just felt lost in the cases, I was literally talking to myself all afternoon imploring myself not to give up, and that I'd (hopefully) done a good job on the comp, so I still had a chance.

I love this email! He has shown us how important it is to know that we are not alone. Just knowing that someone else had gone through the exact same experience and been successful, was a constant reminder to him that he could be successful too. As experienced writers, we feel so much shame that we don't want to advertise our failures! But if we do, we learn that we are not alone.

This candidate clearly worked very diligently at remaining positive all year. This is not an easy task, but you can accomplish anything if you are dedicated, and he was. It is inspiring to hear his story.

In a following email regarding how males and females react differently to the emotions of failing the UFE, and discussing whether men can relate to the emotional aspect of the book, he replied:

Theoretically I don't know why that would be the case. The feelings of embarrassment, initial lack of motivation and talking negatively about oneself would seem similar for both sexes. At the same time I'm thinking every individual, male or female, goes through different emotions in dealing with failing and trying to prepare for the next attempt.

I couldn't agree more. So, to all the male experienced writers who may feel that they shouldn't feel such strong emotions from failing the UFE, please know that you are not alone.

This Student Struggled to Get a Job
But she wasn't about to give up!

I worked with a student that lost her job due to the recession and had to complete almost all of the CASB modules on her own, and to add to the stress her mother's health deteriorated at the beginning of here first UFE attempt. In addition, she didn't have enough articling hours to write the UFE. CASB allowed her to write the UFE, even though she was not working at a firm. It was very stressful because she felt that if she didn't pass the UFE she wouldn't be able to get a job. In addition, all her friends were near the end of their articling experience and would become CA's as soon as they passed, but she had so many hours still to work. Because of this stress, she went overboard while studying for the UFE in 2010, overcompensating for her lack of work experience, and failed.

Did I cry when I realized I failed the UFE. No! Frankly, I was too exhausted for any emotion. By the next day I was planning to write the UFE again, getting a mentor/marker as I knew the study buddy system didn't work for me, and figuring out how to meet the cost of writing the UFE again, since I didn't have a job. One thing I learned about myself was that I was stubborn and didn't take no for an answer."

In reflecting she says:

"So why did I fail UFE?

1. I over reacted and studied more than I was supposed to, including weekends. I thought that if I studied lots I would pass, and passing was my ticket to getting hired and finishing my articling hours. (NOTE: Although she failed in 2010, she did get a job and was employed when she wrote again in 2011!)

2. Failing was not an option for me. I thought, "who will hire me if I fail?" This thought tortured me during those four weeks of UFE study and I focused on that instead of focusing on being positive.

3. I had no support from a firm. I had done six CASB Modules on my own so I thought, "How could the UFE be different?" I was so wrong. I needed support!

4. I was more focused on technical than on my approach to responding to cases. I thought that what I learned in Densmore didn't apply to me, because they didn't realize what I'd gone through and I felt that I was different!

5. *I just read the evaluation guide rather than debriefing the proper way. I didn't learn to properly debrief until 2011 when I wrote my second time, and I realized how little I had learned the year before from simply reading the guide.*

6. *I got burnt out in CASB's Module 6. I was miserable. It had taken so much mental strength to get to this point without support from a firm. But I wasn't worried because I was performing well in Module 6 compared to my peers. But the following weeks continued to ware on me, and by the time I wrote the UFE I was burned out and too tired to properly focus and ultimately pass.*

Although this student didn't pass in 2010, she did find a job! And when she wrote the UFE in 2011 she was more supported because she had a firm and a mentor, and she knew what to expect her second time around. This is a real example of a student getting a job after failing the UFE.

This Student Didn't Know Why She Had Failed
And then she discovered she has reading disabilities

Several students have a hard time passing the UFE as a result of reading disabilities. Try to find someone who did pass the UFE with a reading disability, so that you have someone to talk to who has been through it too. You can email me through my website for contacts at www.KaylaSwitzer.com.

One student I heard from not only had a reading disability, she was also seven months pregnant when she wrote the UFE the second time. Because of her reading disability she wrote in a private room, so the environment was completely different than the first time she wrote the exam. It was calmer for her as she did not have to listen to all the students typing, nor did she have to feel the stressful energy of the exam room. Here is her story.

I was very anxious about writing the UFE again. After failing I didn't know what I could have done differently to pass. I felt that I had done all that I could do the first time I wrote. I really did not know what I would do differently the second time. I had worked very hard in preparing for the exam the first time I wrote, but I had a hard time getting all the information into my response in the time required, which I finally learned was because of a reading disability I hadn't known about.

Reading "I Failed the UFE! Now What?" increased my confidence to seek the support of a psychologist and discuss my struggles with anxiety about the UFE. Through discussion with the psychologist, she and I thought that a learning disability may be the underlying cause of my anxiety around the exam and that this potential disability was preventing me from achieving my goal of passing the UFE.

My psychologist recommended a neuropsychologist who would complete a psych-educational assessment on me to determine if I had a learning disability. I had to go through a day of educational testing and an interview with the neuropsychologist. In the end I was diagnosed with a reading disability, which meant that compared to other thirty year old females my reading skills were below average, and that there was a significant discrepancy between my reading skills and my above average IQ scores. The diagnosis made sense to me as I had always felt that I was a slow reader but I didn't realize that it was preventing me from passing the UFE!

Because of my reading disability, I was provided additional time to write the UFE so that I was able to perform to my maximum potential. I passed the UFE on my second attempt! I will never know for sure what enabled me to pass on my second attempt. Maybe it was the extra time for my reading disability or maybe I finally learned how to "play the game".

This Student Did Not Let Her Emotions Get in the Way
She was positive from day one

I failed the UFE. At first saying that was weird for me, but with time I actually came to embrace the fact that this had happened to me and now I don't even shy away from the fact that it happened.

I first wrote the UFE in the fall of 2009. I did everything I was told. Followed my firms' guidelines for studying, worked my butt off during the day and then allowed myself some time to re-group on evenings and weekends. One thing I didn't fully embrace was making it a summer of studying for ME. My "mothering nature" started to get the best of me towards the end of the summer. I spent a significant amount of additional time helping my study buddies out rather than focusing all of my attention on me. By the time it came to write the UFE... I was burnt out.

The week before marks were released I had a bad feeling. In my gut, I knew I wasn't going to pass long before I actually saw it on paper. UFE marks morning came. My boyfriend (now fiancé) and I woke up and checked. He got online before I did. He passed! Of course we were both over-joyed and thrilled by this news. Then I checked... ugh. At the time, I'm not sure what was worse. The reality of knowing I hadn't passed or knowing that I put such a damper on his day. (Side note: I insisted that my boyfriend leave that morning & treat the day as his. Enjoy it! Embrace it! I didn't want him to miss out on this just because of me and if I had to re-live that morning I wouldn't change a thing).

I absorbed the news that morning. I called my parents and cried a little. But that was it. After I got off the phone I felt like my entire attitude changed about the exam. Screw it! Regardless of not knowing why exactly I faltered (at that time) I was even more determined to re-write and kill it the following year. Not attempting it again was never an option.

I went into work the following week and confronted the issue head-on. I sent an email to some colleagues stating that yes it was true; I didn't make it this time, but thank you for their support and words of encouragement. Most importantly I wanted to let everyone know that I wasn't someone that they needed to walk on egg-shells around at the office. I would say that the majority of people really don't know how to act after you tell them you have failed the UFE. That's why I sent the message to let everyone know I was okay and to just move on (like I had already done).

What really amazed me was how quickly the stories came out from the woodwork that "Oh, well you know John Smith right? He re-wrote twice and now is the CFO of XYZ Company." You'd be amazed at how many of the most successful people today have turned this event around and gone on to become extremely successful.

Some time went on and I obtained my detailed evaluation (PAR). My downfall was one sentence in the exam that year. I failed because of ONE sentence. At first it killed me when I found this out. That feeling lasted for 30 seconds. I wasn't going to get angry at the process or the exam or the markers. It is what it is. Deal with it, learn from it and move on. That was my attitude for the year.

I started channeling every other resource I could to find out how successful experienced writers had attacked the summer. Kayla was a huge help to me and I picked her brain a ton prior to finalizing my plan for studying. I spoke with people that approached studying in a variety of ways whether it be alone, with a buddy or in a group. I just gathered a ton of information (like any Type A accountant would do), assessed all of my options and made a decision based on this analysis that would be right for ME.

As I said before, in hindsight I realized that my mothering nature distracted me and caused me to not be as selfish as I should have been. I spent that little extra time helping others out which lead to my burn out. That burn out resulted in my skimming over the infamous sentence in the COMP, the one sentence that caused me to fail the UFE. (Remember that every sentence in the exam is there for a reason. You just need to figure out why! A lesson I learned the hard way.) So with this new information in hand, I decided to tackle my next summer of studying alone.

I was able to do this as I work best in this environment. I had previously thrived in the CASB environment as I had also done when I obtained my high school diploma from a similarly structured environment. Working independently was the best fit for me, knowing that I had a multitude of additional resources if I needed any help. I am also my own worst critic. Knowing that, I arranged to have a wide variety of co-workers mark questions for me throughout the summer (note: I only asked co-workers that I knew had either (a) experience marking cases previously for our firm or (b) had actually marked the UFE). I ensured that I was getting at least two questions marked each week. I would also mark it of course, and compare it to theirs. I found this gave me a really good gauge on whether I was being too hard or not on myself.

Two challenges faced faced that summer were (a) trying not to study again too soon and (b) dealing with my boyfriend. On the first challenge... my words of advice are that the information comes back A LOT quicker. You are already ten steps ahead of the other writers because you know the difference between a Multi and a Comp, you already have all of the information buried in your head... you just need a refresher. So don't be tempted to dive back into it again too quickly.

Now for the second challenge. Just like everyone else, he really had a difficult time trying to figure out what he could do or should be doing to help me out. Yes, I will admit that me rewriting the UFE put a strain on our relationship. But that was only until I figured out what his role should be throughout the year and summer. He had the best intentions whenever he asked me questions at the beginning, but it wasn't what I needed. So I tasked him to keep me entertained and distracted. We were not allowed to talk about the UFE in the evenings (unless I needed a major venting session for a moment of two) and he was responsible for keeping me active or getting me out of the house, whether or not I wanted to. This worked amazingly well. I had my biggest fan supporting me but in a totally different way. He may not realize what an impact it had, but having him around to keep me sane (and not involved in seeing my progress, etc) was key in helping me kick butt.

That brings me to the end of my story, to September 2010 when I re-wrote the UFE. This time I didn't have gross feelings walking out each day. I went in feeling energized and ready to tackle each question head on.

Two of the highlights from the day marks were released are (a) seeing my study buddies from the previous year waiting at the office when I walked in the door and the massive hugs I got from them that day, and (b) calling my dad (a fellow CA) to let him know I kicked butt this time!

This such a positive story, from a student who knew exactly what she needed and didn't let her emotions get in the way. This is the perfect example of a very strong experienced writer!

A Third Time Writer's Story
When the traditional study plan doesn't work

Sometimes what works for everyone else doesn't work for you. Nobody will know that but you, so you need to take charge so that you can pass the UFE. This student worked so hard to pass on her third attempt and made changes in everything she did, and she passed! Here is what she did to make sure she passed on her third attempt.

The third time I wrote I wrote at a smaller location in Burnaby instead of Vancouver, because Vancouver was too overwhelming with all the hype.

I ditched all the "advice" that I was always told was the only way I could pass the UFE, such as I HAVE to have a study partner, I HAVE to do two multi's a day, I HAVE to study from 9 a.m. to 5 p.m. I ignored the suggested study "time frame" and started organizing stuff in April/May so I felt comfortable. I wrote one multi a day and debriefed until I was comfortable. Two was too many for me. I went back to what I was comfortable with; learning on my own. I started out with a study partner, but we only sat at the same table and wrote together for motivation. I did not mark her stuff and made it clear I didn't want mine marked by her. I think it's a huge waste of time for two people who don't know what they're doing to be marking. Instead, I hired a professional who I called every day and went over every single multi and comp with. This was part of my debrief.

I cut out all the negatives in my life. I stopped hanging out with a friend who said that my "UFE stuff" was too much to handle, and that I had changed as a result of failing. I told work I wasn't going to deal with work and stress, so I took off a lot of time off throughout the year to get my head "in the game."

I told myself every single day that I would pass. I went as far as changing all of my passwords to "IwillpassUFE" and "UFEsuccess", so I was reminded of it daily and constantly.

I exercised every single day, ate healthy every single day, spent time with people who encouraged me every day.

I stopped ignoring my weaknesses. I realized with one week to write that I DID NOT KNOW HOW TO APPROACH ASSURANCE! I called up my marker and he walked me through it. It was so embarrassing to go to him and say "I don't get this...after three years. Here I am, and I need help." But I bit the bullet, and I am so grateful I did. I also spent a lot of time analyzing my responses to figure out what I constantly did poorly on. And I started to really see what I didn't understand. I knew conceptually what I was supposed to write, but I didn't know HOW. For example, an audit memo. Easy, right? Turns out I didn't know how to write the R of RAMP for risk, so I never got the points in it. So I sat down with my fiance for literally hours writing out example after example until the light went on! I finally got it! I constantly felt like lights were going on in my third UFE summer.

I got rid of all the UFE notes and turned the UFE process into one page of notes, so that I wasn't thinking "OH MY GOD. THERE IS SO MUCH!"

At the end of the day, the reason I passed was that I started ignoring all of the advice out there and went with my gut. Why? I finally realized that I graduated at the top of my class in high school, I got into one of the best universities and into one of the hardest programs, I survived four years of articling at a CA firm while having failed twice. If I could do all that, why was I ignoring my gut about what was right FOR ME to pass the

UFE.

But the biggest thing was confidence. The third year I had confidence. I gained it by preparing the way that I felt comfortable and by staying engaged. I cut out all the negative attitude and thoughts like "This sucks!" "Why me?" "It's so hard!" "I can't do it!" I had hard days, for sure. I would go crying to my fiance and to my marker. During Day Two I was panicking a bit. Then I stopped. I just went back to what I knew, like the approaches that I practiced, my outline, and just slotted my knowledge into it. I just thought, "Here's what I know, and here's what the technique is."

This is the perfect example of someone who had to ignore the traditional study plan, accept that it wasn't right, and take control to pass the UFE!

Thank you to everyone who emailed me asking questions and sharing their experiences all summer long. I love hearing from you!

Contact

If you need a mentor, a marker or just an ear to listen, please always feel free to contact me through my website at **www.KaylaSwitzer.com**.

Follow my blog at **KaylaSwitzer.wordpress.com** and **Like it on Facebook** "I Failed the UFE! Now What?"

Are you an experienced writer? Want to be part of this book next year? I'd love to hear your story! In fact, I would love to hear your thoughts, suggestions, and questions at anytime during your UFE experience.

Email me through my website at www.KaylaSwitzer.com

"Nothing is predestined: The obstacles of your past can become the gateways that lead to new beginnings."

- Ralph Blum -
Writer and Cultural Anthropologist

"What is defeat? Nothing but education; nothing but the first steps to something better."

– Proverb –

IN CONCLUSION....

I know how it feels to have to rewrite the UFE, but to feel the pride and accomplishment of passing is worth every moment of the effort I put into my second summer. If I can do it, you can too!

Reread it as much as you need to during the year to ensure that you are always working towards passing, and that you aren't falling behind. This book will guide you from December when you fail to passing the following year, with all the highs and lows along the way. This book is for you. It is a resource of information based on my personal experiences. Use it to its full potential.

Believe in yourself. I believe in you!

> "After my house burned down, I could
> see the moon more clearly."
> - Zen saying -

NOTES

The story about Amadou Diallo and the temporary autism discussion in Chapter Three comes from Gladwell, Malcolm. "Seven Seconds in the Bronx: The Delicate Art of Mind Reading." Blink. New York: Hachette Book Group USA, 2005. 189-244.

Descriptions of people following their quotes were all found on HYPERLINK http://www.Wikipedia.org www.Wikipedia.org.

The example of a Performance Analysis Report in Chapter Three is based on an example at www.icao.on.ca www.icao.on.ca.

In addition to obtaining the numbers for the flow-through rate, on several occasions throughout the book I mention Densmore, Bruce. UFE Success...Mastering Competency-Based Testing. Nova Scotia: Densmore Consulting Services (DCS) Inc, 2008. See also www.dcsweb.ca.

The story about the CA who became a doctor comes from Stefenac, Rosalind. "The Professional." CA Magazine November 2007.

"Success is sweet: the sweeter if long delayed and attained through manifold struggles and defeats."
- A. Branson Alcott -
American teacher, writer, and philosopher

ACKNOWLEDGMENTS

Thank you to my family for your support. You always have an extraordinary belief in me. Thank you for understanding when I failed the UFE, for celebrating when I passed it, and for editing this book. (Thank you to Bree especially. I am so grateful for your hours and hours of editing!)

To Todd, who wrote the UFE as many times as I did (in theory!) but can laugh at it all the same. Thank you for keeping me laughing, for suggest- ing this book, and for being more excited than I was when I passed. Thank you for supporting me in taking time off (and paying the bills!), for edit- ing, and making suggestions to the end. This book wouldn't have happened without you.

And to Ida Leung. You were the nicest, most dedicated mentor an experienced writer could have. Thank you.

"What will be will be, but now I know, there's an unshakeable seed, at the center of my soul."
- Aspen Switzer -
Singer

Appendix: Study Schedule

March 2012

Sunday	Monday	Tuesday	Wednesday	Thursday	Friday	Saturday
				1	2	3 Write DCS 2011 Non-Comp Simulation
4	5	6	7	8	9	10 Debrief Non-Comp Simulation
11	12	13	14	15	16	17 Study Technical (4-6 hours)
18	19	20	21	22	23	24 Write DCS 2011 Non-Comp Simulation
25	26	27	28	29	30	31 Debrief Non-Comp Simulation

DCS Simulations: Densmore Consulting Services Inc. sells practice simulations at www.DCSWeb.ca based on the prior year UFE.

Study Technical: Prioritize your technical study topics and study by priority. Know the technical that's most important, and study that.

Note: All simulations and technical study are scheduled on the weekend. However, you can break this up as you like between weekdays and weekends.

April 2012

Sunday	Monday	Tuesday	Wednesday	Thursday	Friday	Saturday
1	2	3	4	5	6	7 Study Technical (4-6 hours)
8	9	10	11	12	13	14 Write DCS 2011 Non-Comp Simulation
15	16	17	18	19	20	21 Debrief Non-Comp Simulation
22	23	24	25	26	27	28 Study Technical (4-6 hours)
29	30					

DCS Simulations: Densmore Consulting Services Inc. sells practice simulations at www.DCSWeb.ca based on the prior year UFE.

Study Technical: Prioritize your technical study topics and study by priority. Know the technical that's most important, and study that.

Note: All simulations and technical study are scheduled on the weekend. However, you can break this up as you like between weekdays and weekends.

May 2012

Sunday	Monday	Tuesday	Wednesday	Thursday	Friday	Saturday
		1	2	3	4	5 Study Technical (4-6 hours)
6	7	8	9	10	11	12 Study Technical (4-6 hours)
13	14	15	16	17	18	19 Write DCS 2011 Comprehensive Simulation
20	21	22	23	24	25	26 Debrief Comprehensive Simulation
27	28	29	30	31		

DCS Simulations: Densmore Consulting Services Inc. sells practice simulations at www.DCSWeb.ca based on the prior year UFE.

Study Technical: Prioritize your technical study topics and study by priority. Know the technical that's most important, and study that.

Note: All simulations and technical study are scheduled on the weekend. However, you can break this up as you like between weekdays and weekends.

June 2012

Sunday	Monday	Tuesday	Wednesday	Thursday	Friday	Saturday
					1	2 Study Technical (4-6 hours)
3	4	5	6	7	8	9 Study Technical (4-6 hours)
10	11	12	13	14	15	16 4 hours under exam conditions: 3 DCS 2011 Non-Comp Simulations
17	18	19	20	21	22	23 Debrief Non-Comp Simulations
24	25	26	27	28	29	30

DCS Simulations: Densmore Consulting Services Inc. sells practice simulations at www.DCSWeb.ca based on the prior year UFE.

Study Technical: Prioritize your technical study topics and study by priority. Know the technical that's most important, and study that.

Note: All simulations and technical study are scheduled on the weekend. However, you can break this up as you like between weekdays and weekends.

July 2012

Sunday	Monday	Tuesday	Wednesday	Thursday	Friday	Saturday
1	2	3	4	5	6	7 Study Technical (6-8 hours)
8	9 Experienced Writers Two Day course in Vancouver	10 Experienced Writers Two Day course in Vancouver	11	12	13	14 Study Technical (6-8 hours)
15	16	17	18	19	20 Off!	21
22	23 DCS UFE Prep for experienced writers	24 DCS UFE Prep for experienced writers	25 DCS UFE Prep for experienced writers	26 DCS UFE Prep for experienced writers	27 DCS UFE Prep for experienced writers	28
29 DCS UFE Prep for experienced writers	30 DCS UFE Prep for experienced writers	31				

Experienced Writers Two Day course in Vancouver: This is a two-day course held exclusively for experienced writers by Kayla Switzer. This course is held in Vancouver and covers everything from the emotional aspect of the exam to how to approach cases, including two marked non-comp cases.

DCS Simulations: Densmore Consulting Services Inc. sells practice simulations at www.DCSWeb.ca based on the prior year UFE.

Study Technical: Prioritize your technical study topics and study by priority. Know the technical that's most important, and study that.

Note: All simulations and technical study are scheduled on the weekend. However, you can break this up as you like between weekdays and weekends.

August 2012

Sunday	Monday	Tuesday	Wednesday	Thursday	Friday	Saturday
			1 DCS UFE Prep for experienced writers	2 Off!	3 Off!	4
5	6 Take this week off or easy study.	7 If studying, assemble study materials and/or write two or three cases.	8 If you are writing cases, write 2008 Non-Comp cases in this week.	9	10	11
12	13 2008 Comp. Write and Mark (don't debrief)	14 **Morning**: Debrief Comp **Afternoon**: 2009 Non-Comp	15 **Morning**: 2009 Non-Comp **Afternoon**: 2008 Non-Comp	16 **Morning**: 2008 Non-Comp **Afternoon**: 2009 Non-Comp	17 **Morning**: 2010 Non-Comp **Afternoon**: Flex Friday	18
19	20 2010 Comp. Write and Mark (don't debrief)	21 **Morning**: Debrief Comp **Afternoon**: 2008 Non-Comp	22 **Morning**: 2010 Non-Comp **Afternoon**: 2009 Non-Comp	23 **Morning**: 2009 Non-Comp **Afternoon**: 2010 Non-Comp	24 **Morning**: 2011 Non-Comp **Afternoon**: Flex Friday	25
26	27 2011 Comp. Write and Mark (don't debrief)	28 **Morning**: Debrief Comp **Afternoon**: 2010 Non-Comp	29 **Morning**: 2011 Non-Comp **Afternoon**: 2010 Non-Comp	30 **Morning**: 2011 Non-Comp **Afternoon**: 2011 Non-Comp	31 **Morning**: 2011 Non-Comp **Afternoon**: Flex Friday	

Flex Friday: Work on your weaknesses in the afternoon. Review your tracker and determine what you need to work on.

September 2012

Sunday	Monday	Tuesday	Wednesday	Thursday	Friday	Saturday
						1
2	3 2009 Comp. Write and Mark (don't debrief)	4 **Morning**: Debrief Comp **Afternoon**: 2011 Non-Comp	5 **Morning**: 2010 Non-Comp **Afternoon**: 2009 Non-Comp	6 **Morning**: Recycled Non-Comp **Afternoon**: Flex Day	7 **Morning**: Recycled Non-Comp **Afternoon**: Flex Day	8
9	10	11 UFE	12 UFE	13 UFE	14	15
16	17 Holiday!	18 Holiday!	19 Holiday!	20 Holiday!	21 Holiday!	22
23	24	25	26	27	28	29

Legend
Recycled Non-Comp: Write a case that you have already written that you know you will do well on. Do not do a new case here, or a case you previously didn't do well on because it could be detrimental to your confidence if you don't do well.
Flex Day: Work on your weaknesses in the afternoon. Review your tracker and determine what you need to work on. Work on your confidence. Believe in yourself. You can pass the UFE!

Made in the USA
Charleston, SC
07 February 2014